Eduti…
Restructuring, Technology, and the Future of Education

David D. Thornburg, Ph.D.

Starsong Publications

Thornburg, David D.
Edutrends 2010: Restructuring, Technology, and the Future of Education

ISBN 0-942207-10-6 (pbk.)

ISBN 0-942207-10-6
1 2 3 4 5 6 7 8 9 0

To those who want to see real improvement in American Education, I say: There will be no renaissance without revolution.

President G. Bush
April 18, 1991

The revolution is at hand...

Acknowledgement
From the tale of Prometheus and Native American myths to CD-ROM's and virtual reality, this book mirrors the processes of my mind. As I'm writing these words, I'm sitting in the waiting room of the hospital during my mother's heart surgery (which she came through with flying colors, by the way.)

Something about the personal events of this week makes this an appropriate place to capture thoughts of acknowledgement. We are shaped by our parents and, unless the hill slopes downward, the nut doesn't move far from the tree. My father's hands-on approach to life and technology have shaped me, as has my mother's love of art, story and philosophy. For these reasons, I find it possible to blend ideas of ancient teachers with the technology of today in a form that, I hope, challenges my readers.

Of the teachers in my life – my wife, my son, my parents – there are many to thank. But for now, I'd like to single out just one.

Thank you, mom.

❄ Contents

❄ Introduction

In times of change, learners inherit the earth, while the learned find themselves beautifully equipped to deal with a world that no longer exists.

Eric Hoffer

Futurist commentators have observed that societies undergo rapid transformation during the transition years between centuries. This "end of the century" phenomenon has been with us for a long time. As Marvin Cetron and Owen Davies note in their book, *American Renaissance: Our Life at the Turn of the 21st Century*, the end of the 16th century was punctuated by numerous developments including Shakespeare's sonnets, Cervantes' Don Quixote, and the science of Galileo and Kepler.

Events of similar magnitude mark the transition years of other centuries as well. For example, at the end of the 19th and start of the 20th century, Roentgen discovered X-rays, Planck created the foundations of quantum mechanics, Einstein was hard at work on relativity theory, and Thompson discovered the electron. Technological breakthroughs of the time led to the start of radio and airplanes. Advances of similar magnitude existed in other areas – the Post-Impressionist art movment, the music of Debussy, and so on.

And now that the end of the twentieth century is in sight, rapid change is with us once again. Ten years ago, few would have predicted the demise of the USSR, the unification of Germany, or many of the technologies we now take for granted.

It is appropriate, I think, to note that many of our institutions have changed in the past few decades. ATM's have made banking an activity that customers can perform any time, day or night. The town theater, once restricted to showing a single movie (or double feature) is now likely to be a cineplex showing as many as a dozen or more films at a time. The mom and pop grocery store has turned into the 24-hour supermarket where one can purchase socks, engine oil and light bulbs along with ham and eggs.

About the only institution that looks pretty much the same as it did in our youth is the school house. Many changes have in fact been made in education through the years, but these changes are not obvious to many outside observers, and some schools operate as if the world of the 50's still exists.

As with other institutions, education in the United States is receiving pressure from many quarters to change. Some of this pressure is appropriate, and some of it is not, but the pressure exists just the same. Some of the forces being applied to education are:

Increased public concern:

- "Education bashing" by government and industry leaders is on the rise.

- Parents are asking for "choice" and see publicly funded tuition vouchers as a way to improve public schools by providing more competition from the private sector.

- The government is asking for a uniform national assessment of educational progress, leading to a uniform national curriculum.

Rapidly changing demographics:

- The number of non-English-speaking immigrants is rapidly rising. (In California, for example, this population accounts for 3/4 of the state's new arrivals.)

- One-fifth of the children in the United States live in poverty.

- Child abuse, parental drug abuse and the other problems of our society place extra pressure on educators as their roles expand to become surrogate parents and social workers.

- Growth in single parent families or families

where both parents work places pressure on schools to become extended day-care providers, and cuts down on the number of parents who can assist in their child's classroom.

Rapid changes in technology:

- Banks, grocery stores, theaters, offices and factories have undergone major structural changes in the past four decades yet many schools look and feel the same as they did forty years ago.

- Workers at all levels have access to modern technology. Fax machines are found in virtually all businesses and are starting to show up in American homes. Yet many schools consider themselves lucky if they have a single working copier serving the needs of two dozen teachers and 700 students.

- Information access from the home has grown phenomenally in the past decade. One third of our homes have personal computers in them. Cable and direct broadcast satellite services bring as many as 100 or more channels of television into some homes today, and new information services linking telecommunications and computers have created a global village. Classrooms, on the other hand, all too often exist in isolation from communication with the rest of the world.

- Students of the late 20th century have a completely different world-view from that of their parents. One third of today's students will graduate in the 21st century. None of them has known a time when we were not space travelers. Virtually all of them are comfortable with the rapid pace of change that seems so disequilibrating to many of us.

These forces pull at the fabric of education from many directions. Unless we restructure education in a way that communicates effectively with our youth, schools will simply become irrelevant in the lives of students by the end of the decade.

Our goals...

This book has several goals: First, we will explore the "facts" behind the recent flurry of teacher bashing that is sweeping the nation. We will explore the likely outcome of a voucher-based education and examine some of the tragic flaws in the reasoning of those who would dismantle public education in our country.

Next, we'll explore the change process and the problem of "paradigm paralysis" as it applies to educational restructuring.

Finally, we will explore both the social and technological trends shaping education and propose a way for each of us to think intelligently about the future while we work together to reshape our educational institutions to meet the needs of our society.

Some have argued that it is too late – that our educational system has collapsed and that we must trash it before building a new one from the ashes. While I agree that rapid and revolutionary change is essential, I think we have the brainpower and the will to do the task at hand.

As George Bernard Shaw wrote in his play, *Back to Methuselah*: "You see things; and you say, "Why?" But I dream things that never were; and I say, "Why not?"

❄ Education at Risk

Ever since the publication of the 1983 blue-ribbon education panel report, *A Nation at Risk*, public education has become the whipping boy of American society. In recent years the pace has quickened, culminating with the current attacks on education from American industry and government offices all the way from our local communities to the White House.

What is the cause of this angst? Is public education failing to meet the needs of hyperindustrial society? Have we truly created an educational wasteland filled with students who lack the skills needed to hold even the most menial jobs? Or, is it instead the case that we are being attacked unfairly – that we are doing a better job than we are being given credit for. If this is the case then we must ask an even more chilling question – why are powerful forces amassing to destroy the fabric of public education, the cornerstone of our democracy?

To get some insight into these questions, there is no better starting point than the *America 2000* document distributed by Education Secretary Lamar Alexander's office. This document suggests that effective educational restructuring should be centered around the six goals created at the 1990 Governor's conference on education. These six goals are listed below:

By the year 2000:

1. All children in America will start school ready to learn.

2. The high school graduation rate will increase to at least 90%.

3. American students will leave grades four, eight, and twelve having demonstrated competency in challenging subject matter including English, mathematics, science, history, and geography; and every school in America will ensure that all students learn to use their minds well, so they may be prepared for responsible citizenship, further learning, and productive employment in our modern economy.

4. U.S. students will be first in the world in science and mathematics achievement.

5. Every adult American will be literate and will possess the knowledge and skills necessary to compete in a global economy and exercise the rights and responsibilities of citizenship.

6. Every school in America will be free of drugs and violence and will offer a disciplined environment conducive to learning.

States and individual schools districts are being asked to use these goals as the foundation for educational reform – and, in many cities and state houses across the country, leaders are falling all over themselves in a rush to jump on the America 2000 bandwagon.

If we are to use a set of goals as a premise for restructuring, these goals should be carefully examined first. Do they point to a clearly defined major mission for education? If so, what is it? If not, shouldn't we resolve this topic first? I'll have more to say about this later.

Second, if these goals are worthwhile, how are we doing? This is the question we'll explore now.

Dropping out is hard to do

When I first saw this list, I wondered why the graduation goal for the year 2000 was 90% – why not 95%, or 87.3%? I found the answer when the Department of Education sent, at my request, the national graduation rates since 1910. These rates show the percentage of 24-year-olds who had graduated from high school or otherwise demonstrated equivalent proficiency. A plot of this data is shown below.

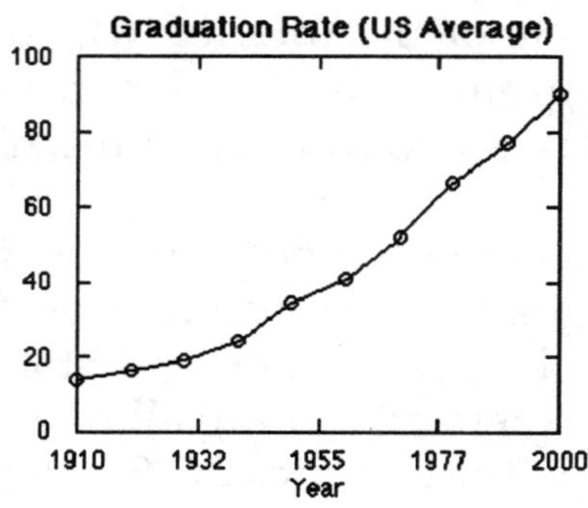

There are a few things to notice about this graph. First, the graduation rate hovered around 20% or so until World War II, at which point it started a steady rise – virtually unbroken – up to 1990. In fact, if you extend the straight line through the 1990 point (as we have in the graph), the line hits the 90% graduation rate by the year 2000. In other words, we have been right on target for a 90% graduation rate in the year 2000 since the end of World War II.

As I was making this plot, another thought came to mind. If, instead of graduation rate, we published the Dow Jones average, would you be able to identify the onset of the depression, or more recent economic downturns? Of course. These crashes show up in sharp declines in the market. Now, looking instead at the graduation rate chart, can you identify the equivalent crash in education leading to the *Nation at Risk* document in 1983? Of course not. The fact is that the graduation rate for our country has never been higher than it is now, and our progress in making it better has been steady for about 50 years.

What conclusions can we draw from this? Either we

must conclude that graduation rate has little to do with academic excellence (in which case the 90% goal is a meaningless target), or that we have been doing a great job at moving steadily toward this goal for the past 50 years (in which case the 90% goal is a meaningless target).

There is a third alternative – that we are being bushwhacked into thinking that our educational system is in ruins so it can be taken over by those with special agendas. This possibility will be addressed later.

Of course it is possible that we are graduating a nation of dunces – that a high-school diploma is no indicator of mastery. To examine this hypothesis, let's look at post secondary education.

According to *Perspectives on Education in America,* an unpublished report from Sandia National Laboratories, 57% of all American 18 to 19 year-olds attempt post secondary studies. This number has been steadily increasing since the 1970's and it is twice the percentage of Japanese students who even attempt college. 26% of our youth will receive bachelor's degrees – a number equal to the percentage of Japanese students who simply try post secondary education.

I think it is safe to conclude that the high school graduation rate is increasing on target for the 90% goal by year 2000, and that our students are educated well enough to succeed in college.

That brings the number of goals down to five. Next, let's look at the goal of making the United States number one in math and science by the year 2000. Is this a worthy goal? If so, how are we doing?

Rocket scientists or space cadets – you be the judge
According to a study by the International Association for the Evaluation of Educational Achievement described in a 1989 article in Time Magazine, ninth graders in the United States ranked 14th in science when measured against ninth graders in numerous other countries.

The recently released IAEP (International Assessment of Educational Progress) test scores for 1991 paint a similar picture. These results imply that US math and science education stinks when compared against a list of countries including South Korea, Taiwan, Switzerland, Hungary, the former Soviet Union, Slovenia, Italy, Israel, Canada, France, Scotland and Spain. And just how bad are we? Well, South Korea pulled in a 79% average score on the test while we scored 67%. In other words, the gap between the best score and ours was only 12 percentage points.

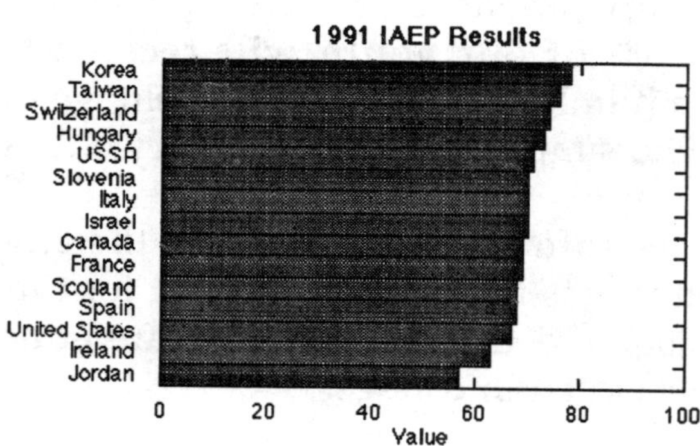

There are some details to consider – the Israeli's

(beating us by 3%) only tested kids in the Hebrew schools where most parents are highly educated, many with advanced degrees in science or engineering. None of the nations who beat us has the heterogeneous population we have, or if it does, the test was given to only a homogeneous subset of the whole. (Only urban Russian-speaking children were tested in the former USSR, for example.)

If we want all our kids to measure up against only the best and brightest the world has to offer, so be it. After all, we're America, land of the free, home of the brave, and the country where our hottest toy is a piñata in the shape of a school.

In other words, the results of this test (and others) were intentionally presented to show us in the worst possible light.

Many international studies are flawed because they examine children in school – immediately invalidating any conclusions that might be drawn. Now, if this sentence leaves you puzzled, let me explain. Of the countries listed in some of the high school studies, very few have ALL high school aged students in a general academic track (or even in school). By the time children reach high school age, only the academically successful are still in the kinds of schools we have in our country. For example, Brazilian high school students score higher than our students in both math and science (according to some studies). Having worked in Brazil, I found this staggering, but explainable. The dropout rate in Brazil is 80%. 60% of Brazilian children drop out at the end of 1st grade. By the time children reach their teens, only the most academically inclined are still in school.

In other words, some of the test results comparing our students with those of other nations compare all our children against only the best and brightest of the other countries. That's like pitting a community touch football team against the San Francisco 49er's.

Short of gathering children off the streets so we can test the whole range of a population, what other measure can we use to see how we match up on the world arena in science? I would suggest looking at Nobel prizes.

The graph below shows Nobel prizes in science by nation up until 1987. As you can see, the United States leads the world, with the U.K. coming in a distant second.

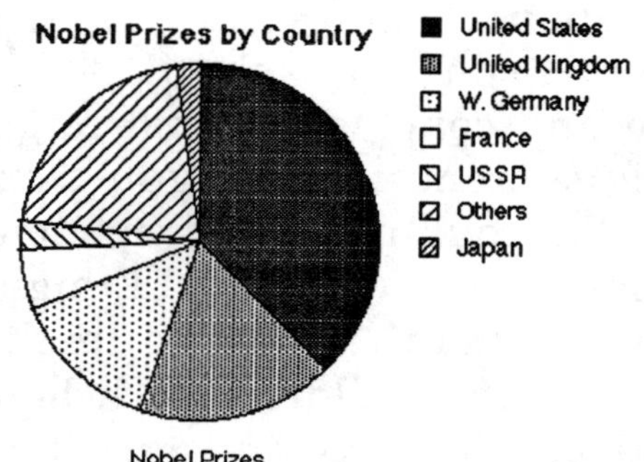

But suppose this achievement measures past achievement; isn't it important to see if we are losing our lead? Well, the next graph, plotting Nobel prizes in science in 15-year segments (excepting for the last segment), shows the United States running away from the pack. Countries like Germany – once leaders in this area – have virtually disappeared from the arena. And Japan has so few Nobel prizes that the country barely deserves mention.

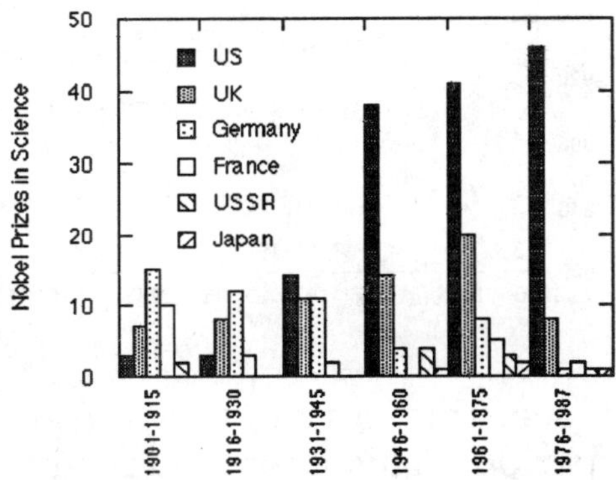

I fail to see how anyone looking at this data (which you can find in an almanac) could fail to accept that the United States is the world leader in science, period.

And what of those countries that do have most of their children in school, but who perform better on the science and math tests than we do? Where are the Nobel prizes in science for Slovenia, Spain or South Korea? If we aren't doing well in science tests, our overwhelming contributions to science are the best case of overachievement I've ever seen.

If our science education is so bad, why are our colleges filled with nationals from other countries who leave their homeland for a quality American education?

One valid criticism of the Nobel Prize data is that it reflects on our educational system of the past, not on the system we have today. That is a fair criticism, so let's look at our test scores today. The chart below shows the average SAT scores for the period from 1965 to 1990.

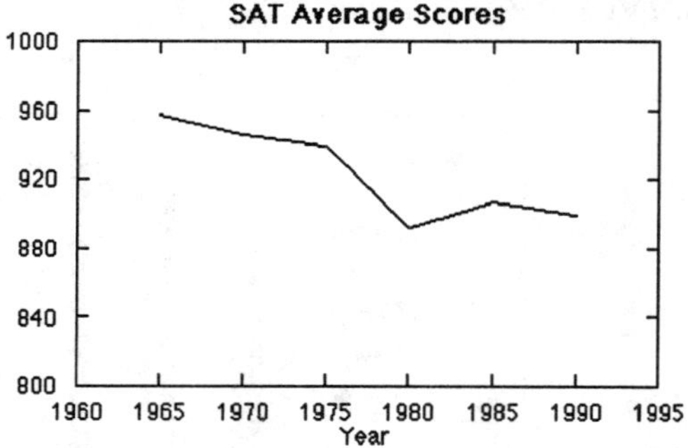

As you can see, this curve shows a general decline during this period. This apparent decline has resulted in considerable education bashing by people as prominent as the President of the United States.

One must be careful before jumping to conclusions, though. The SAT is a voluntary test and there is no control over the mix of students who attempt it. To see why this is important, look at the following figure showing SAT scores based on high school rank.

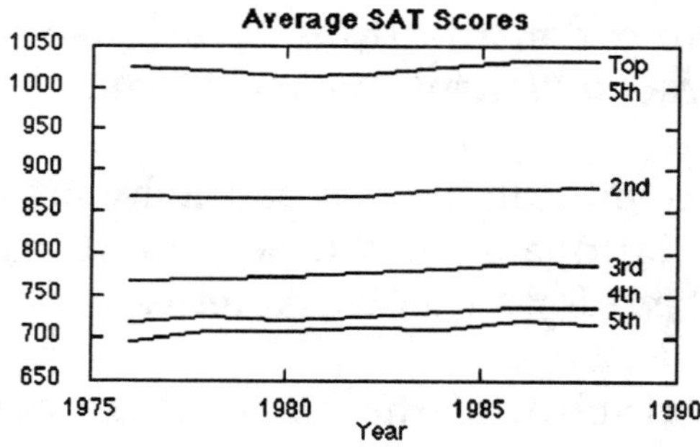

This chart shows a slight increase in test scores for each quintile of the high school class. If each quintile shows improvement then the only explanation for the overall decline is that more students from the lower quintiles of their high school class are now taking this test than ever before.

The next figure shows what happens if we hold the population constant.

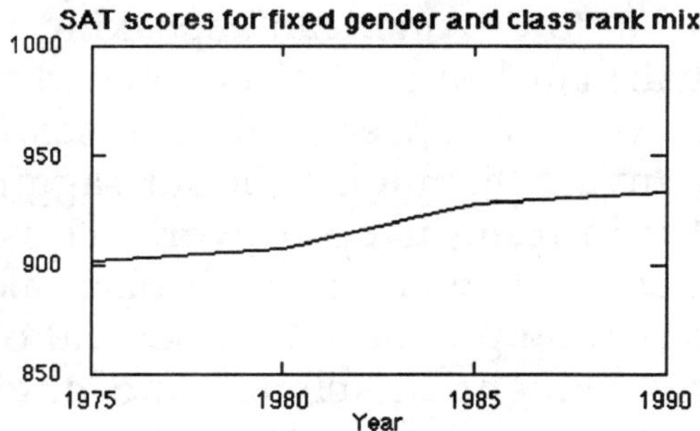

Fixing on the gender and class rank mix of 1975, we see that the scores have actually gone up for this group, confirming that the perceived decline is determined by the class rank and gender mix of student populations taking the test, not by the quality of our educational system. (Gender is an issue only to the extent that the SAT may favor male students.)

The issue of excellence in science is important – I don't want to suggest otherwise, but many people say "science" when they mean technology – two vastly different subjects. Even in technology one would be hard pressed to say that we are not leaders. We invented the digital computer (with due apologies to England's Dr. Babbage); we invented the transistor; we invented the microprocessor; we invented the video tape recorder; we invented the laser video disc; we invented most of the technologies that entertain, educate, and help us manage our businesses – even if the devices that perform these tasks bear labels from other countries.

The problem is not our creativity, our engineering, nor our science. If anywhere, the problem lies in decisions made by corporate America. For example, in 1990, in the midst of a "buy American" speaking tour, former Chrysler chairman Lee Iacocca negotiated an order for $44 million worth of sheet metal presses from Japan, rather than invest this money in our sagging machine tool industry to bring it up to world class standards. These Japanese tools will take their place alongside the German presses he purchased for several other plants. All our achievement in science and engineering is meaningless if one of our most "pro-American" spokespersons purchases his machine tools from abroad rather than investing his company's money here.

When American motives are based on short term profits and greed, we will be whipped economically by those who take the long-term view and invest in the future. For example, Jacques Attali reports that 30 years ago Japan had no machine tool industry, and the US controlled 25% of the world market. Today the US has 5% of the market and Japan has 22%. As long as American companies continue to complain about foreign competition, while purchasing foreign products themselves, "improvement" in science education is meaningless.

Education becomes a convenient scapegoat for those companies who would rather take pot shots at others than deal with their own failure of vision.

Through the looking glass

While science education should continue to be emphasized, (and properly funded), any rational person would have to agree that we have already achieved the science goal created by the Governors for the year 2000. That leaves four goals to go.

Let's look at another one – that our schools be drug and violence free by the year 2000. I applaud this goal, even if I can't see why this topic is education's responsibility alone. Blaming schools for drugs and violence is a lot like blaming banks for being robbed. Schools are mirrors of the community – violence in the community leads to violence in the schools; drug use in the community leads to drug use in schools.

Teachers have enough on their minds dealing with the day-to-day realities of today's school child – sexual abuse, parental neglect, poverty, and so on, without being expected to repair these social ills during the small amount of time allocated to the typical school day. As the Rev. Jesse Jackson once said, the war on drugs won't be meaningful until it moves from the capital of Columbia to the capital of the United States.

In the realm of adult literacy the national goal is nothing less than perfection: 100% adult literacy by the year 2000. How are we doing? According to Dr. Diane Ravitch, Assistant Secretary of Education, the adult literacy rate in the United States is 95%. She revealed this on January 21, 1992 in response to an attack on American education from abroad. Isn't it curious that Washington defends us against foreign bashing, but remains silent when education's critics are homegrown?

What does it mean to be educated in the 21st century?

This is a question that has been given very little attention in the popular press. Perhaps the decision to build a restructuring program around six well-intentioned, if somewhat questionable, goals is designed to take the place of careful debate on the needs of students in 21st century society. This failure to create a long-range vision is tragic.

This much is clear: we cannot test our way to success. The National Assessment of Educational Progress has shown very little change in academic achievement in the past two decades, even though more children are staying in school, and the number of recent non-English speaking immigrants has increased.

I am a strong believer in educational restructuring, but not for the reasons given in the six America 2000 goals.

Our students must be prepared for life in the next century – a time of unprecedented change. The global changes of 1991 will pale in comparison to those that yet face us, and the key to thriving in the new world order is for all of us to become lifelong learners who have retained our native creativity and who know how to use information technologies effectively.

These requirements can't be met with breast-beating and teacher bashing. They can only be met by providing excellent facilities, tools, and teachers – all of which cost money.

And yet, even with an acknowledgement that massive improvement in physical plants, technology, and staff development is required, communities and states from coast to coast have slashed funding for public education.

Meanwhile, some business leaders berate public education for not doing its job. If industry is truly concerned about the educational needs of workers in the 21st century (as it must be), then, since 75% of the people working in industry in the first decade of the next century are already employed, we might ask how corporate America spends it own training dollars. With the exception of the Xerox's, IBM's and other notable companies, corporate America spends a paltry amount on worker training – except for executives. What can we conclude from this? Either workers received just the education they needed when they were in school, or corporations are unwilling to invest in their own people. In either case, the educational concerns of some corporate leaders – while of value to those of us designing educational futures for this country – smack of hypocrisy.

For example, in an article appearing in the Harvard Business Review, Nan Stone states that Japanese auto workers receive 300 hours of training in their first six months, and ours receive only 50.

One of the reasons that this book explores the year 2010 is that, even if our educational system rebuilt itself tomorrow, this new system would impact, at most, one out of five workers in the year 2000. We must take a longer-term view for our children and encourage industry to invest in its own shorter-term interests.

❄ What Does Business Want from Education?

Much of the pressure for educational reform is coming from the American business community. It is easy to dismiss business' criticism of education as an attempt to place the blame for our ills on schools. After all, if schools aren't providing students with the skills they need to survive in the marketplace, our corporations will lose out in international competition.

In fact there are some business leaders who use both education bashing and Japan bashing as a two-pronged attempt to deflect attention away from poor business decisions made by highly compensated executives. This mean-spirited attack on education was described in the previous chapter; and while we may expect such attacks to continue (after all, who wouldn't like to have handy scapegoat to blame for our poor performance in the international marketplace), they mask a more reasoned and supportive concern about our educational system.

Leaders of the National Alliance of Business (NAB) have created a report: *The Business Roundtable Participation Guide: A Primer for Business on Education.* This document, while prone to some of the same misinformation found in our daily newspapers, presents a sensitive and reasonable description of the challenges that face us, and some of the things business can do to help effect positive change in our country's educational system. Unlike many reports on education, this one was written with the aid of educational leaders who have a firm grasp of the situation.

The NAB recognizes that our educational system is doing the best job it has ever done. More people are graduating than ever before; more students are going to college, and so on. The problem as they see it is not that schools have been doing a bad job, but that the world outside the classroom has changed dramatically and education has not changed to meet the needs of today's society.

In order to remain competitive in the marketplace, 23% of our corporations are converting to new forms of production, 3% are moving their production facilities off-shore and 70% are lowering wages or benefits. Low wages hit the high school graduates the hardest. In the past 15 years, high school graduates have seen their earnings drop 24% in constant dollars, while college graduates saw their income increase by 36% in the same time period.

This shrinking of the middle class is the sign of a nation headed to third-world status. Improved education (both in the classroom and on the plant floor) can reverse this trend.

Where has the competitive pressure come from?

Fifteen years ago there were 9 industralized nations. There are now 23, and they all want to compete effectively with us in the international marketplace. Job skills of the past required punctuality, ability to follow directions, and blind obedience to authority. As businesses flatten their management hierarchies in order to speed the response to competitive pressure, all employees need new skills – creativity, flexibility, and tolerance for ambiguity, to name a few. As someone once observed, our schools are perfectly equipped to prepare students for life in the industrial age, but the industrial age no longer exists.

So what does the NAB want?

The NAB has identified nine components for a successful education system, and, while we might quibble about a few of them, this list makes interesting reading.

First, the NAB makes four operating assumptions:

- All students can learn at significantly higher levels.
- We already know how to teach all students effectively.
- Curriculum content must reflect high

expectations for all students, but instructional time and strategies may vary to insure success.
- Every child must have an advocate.

In helping all children to achieve at higher levels, we have to rethink the concept of failure. Schools must not abandon children, but must provide opportunities for them to learn – to develop mastery by supporting them with high expectations and assessment tools that measure what students do know, rather than penalize them for what they don't know.

As for knowing how to teach children effectively, the literature is rich with pedagogical breakthroughs that can be applied in classrooms throughout the country. The problem is not that effective instructional methods don't exist. It is that these powerful tools are hidden from teachers by a system that fails to provide meaningful staff development.

The shift in curriculum must be toward a rigorous curriculum for all, not a watered down curriculum for some. This does not mean that all students should be approached in the same manner. The goal should be to insure that each student learns in his or her best manner. Again, this requires a level of teacher support far beyond that commonplace in schools today.

The importance of advocates for each child cannot be overstated. School objectives require support at home in order to be effective. Children need to know that education is valued by those whose opinions the child trusts. If parental support is non-existent, then an advocate must be found in the extended family, or in the child's community.

(One strikingly successful model for community support is the Intergenerational Program created by John Gill School and the Veteran's Memorial Senior Center in Redwood City, California. During the seven years this program has been in place, students and seniors have formed bonds of mutual support that, in some cases, can't be found at home.)

Second, the NAB wants the new system to be performance or outcome based. All too often teachers focus on inputs ("Here's what I tried.") rather than outcomes ("Here's what worked.") This must change in a world where we expect every child to learn effectively.

Third, assessment strategies must be as strong and as rich as the outcomes. This means that we must move away from assessments that measure a child's capacity to regurgitate information, and move toward assessments that measure reasoning skills, problem solving strategies, and the capacity to integrate ideas from several areas into the solution of a problem.

This also means a move away from the "bubble sheet" standardized tests that comprise the bulk of standardized testing in this country.

There is truth to the adage: "What gets tested gets taught." Assessment needs to keep up with the restructuring of the curriculum, or no meaningful changes will be made.

Fourth, school success should be rewarded and failure penalized. This emphasis on accountability needs to be sensitive to the school's client base. Otherwise we risk comparing children who have supportive home environments and well-equipped schools with those from impoverished homes and underfunded schools. Of all the NAB recommendations, this is one that has to be watched quite closely.

Fifth, school-based staff should have a major role in making instructional decisions. The move toward site-based management is sweeping the nation. The NAB correctly concludes that it is unfair to hold educators responsible for student achievement without empowering them to make decisions and secure the resources needed to do the job. In addition to having school staff choose their managment team, they need to have significant budgetary control as well.

Sixth, major emphasis needs to be placed on staff development. Preservice training needs to be revamped to insure that all new teachers are up to date on the effective use of technology and are aware of the many ways students learn.

Teachers already on the job need to have access to the practical results of educational research. This staff development effort must be ongoing and teachers should be paid for their participation.

The NAB also wants to see alternative certification processes that would allow, for example, early retirees from industry to bring their expertise into the classroom.

Seventh, a high-quality pre-kindergarten needs to be created, especially for disadvantaged students. While no one program holds all the answers, Head Start has shown many positive long-term benefits including improved academic success, reduction in teen pregnacy, drug abuse, and criminal behavior. Programs of this type must be strengthened.

Eighth, health and other social services need to be sufficient to reduce barriers for learning. Increased expectations for our children are meaningless unless we also insure that every mother has high-quality pre-natal care, our children are well nourished, and that our schools are places where children feel safe.

This goal requires unprecedented support from numerous agencies and organizations.

Ninth, technology needs to be used to raise student and teacher productivity and to expand access to learning. The computer will never replace the role of human contact in education, but technology has many other uses. (Universal access to educational technologies of all types is so important that several chapters of this book are devoted to this topic.)

What will business do to support change?
These goals sound quite grand, but just what is business willing to do to help implement them?

As part of the Business Roundtable report, Ernest Boyer listed six areas in which business can help educators achieve their goals. These include:

- Public advocacy
- Renewing people
- Technology as a teaching tool
- Research and Development
- Experiment and Innovate
- Family policy in business must be changed

Let's start with public advocacy. While it is true that, as a group, business leaders don't know any more about education than the public at large, they can provide a powerful force for change. By speaking out on the issues (after learning what the problems really are), business leaders can help focus debate and can provide support to exemplary educational programs by drawing attention to those unsung heroes who create miracles in the classroom every day, but never receive a word of thanks for their effort.

Second, businesses can help teachers renew their skills by offering scholarships for teacher sabbaticals, picking up the tab to send teams of teachers to professional conferences, and underwriting in-house staff development programs. Several projects along these lines have been in place for years, and they pay handsome dividends.

Business can also help preservice institutions beef up their programs through donations, the creation of endowed chairs, etc.

Third, technology is commonplace in industry, but is virtually absent from schools. As Bank Street College's Alan Collins says, "You don't teach people to drive cars by having them ride bicycles." Industry can do a lot to help schools get the technology they need, and to use it effectively. For starters, industry can donate used equipment to schools as it upgrades to newer technologies. Ultimately, schools need to have the same quality of technology found in the world of commerce and industry. Schools should be knocking on the corporate door for assistance in this important area.

Fourth, research and development in education must be well-funded. While government R&D grants should continue, business needs to contribute to this effort as well.

Fifth, business needs to help those schools who are experimenting with new educational strategies. Most schools have no money to fund experimental programs, and industry could help in this arena very easily.

Finally, business needs to provide release time for employees to attend conferences with their children's teachers, just as they do for jury duty or voting. Beyond this, industry can provide extended release time for parents who want to volunteer in their child's classroom. Without this level of support, industry's concern about our educational system lacks commitment.

❄ Vouchers and the Death of Public Education

Some business leaders (and Education Secretary Alexander) suggest that schools will improve if they are forced to compete on the open market. The premise behind this assumption is both fallacious and dangerous.

As I see it, voucher proponents believe that:

- School quality is reflected in test scores
- Parents should be entitled to send their children to any school they choose
- Private schools provide better education that public schools
- Competition will improve public schools

Let's look at these beliefs one at a time, starting with the idea that school quality can be determined from test scores.

The fallacy behind this argument can be heard across the country as leaders of industry speak to educators. Businessmen like David Kearns and Lee Iacocca claim that if their industry produced the level of "damaged goods" produced by education, they would be out of business. Business leaders cite poor scores on the basic math and writing tests given to incoming employees even though, as Nan Stone points out in an article appearing in the Harvard Business Review, many of the things being tested have no bearing on the employee's job.

The fallacy behind the "students as damaged goods" argument is obvious to any educator – children are not the "product" of education, they are education's customers. The curriculum is the product. It is risky to blame schools for poor achievement without looking at the community served by the school.

Many of the schools with the poorest test scores are located in lower income neighborhoods with few financial resources and a larger than average population of children "at-risk" (a euphemism applying to battered children, coke babies, children of poverty, and a growing number of non-English speaking children whose parent(s) (rarely two at home) have little formal education and lack an understanding of the importance of education in their children's lives.) If you really want to see what is happening in our schools, read Jonathan Kozol's *Savage Inequalities*. Read it, and weep.

I live in California. My county contains several school districts whose funding for education varies between districts by almost a factor of two. The poorest district has over 50% minority representation in its schools, and a significant number of these children live in virtual poverty. By contrast, a wealthy neighboring district, already spending thousands more per child, felt that its classrooms were too crowded, so the parents – on their own – raised enough extra money to reduce class size.

There are teachers in the poor district who could teach stones to talk. They are dedicated professionals, some of whom have even sheltered homeless children in their homes. To blame these teachers for producing low test scores is an insult. Before we rush headlong into vouchers, let's swap some teachers from the rich and poor districts and see how they'd do. I'd put my money on the success of the inner-city teachers every time. This isn't to say the teachers in wealthy districts aren't competent – they are. But how many teachers do you know who would jump at the chance to teach in a classroom with a leaky roof and over 50% non-English speaking students spread across six languages?

Next, let's look at the idea that parents should be entitled to send their children to any school they wish.

To hear many voucher supporters talk, you'd think that America's private schools are sitting around waiting for kids to show up at their doors. Vouchers, it is argued, will make it easier for parents to bring kids to private schools since they can be used to offset part of the private school tuition. (California's proposed voucher program would provide about $2500 per child.) This would cover only a fraction of most private schools' tuition, and parents would have to make up the difference themselves.

In most cases, parents do not get to choose to send their children to private schools any more than you or I could "choose" to enroll at Harvard next week. If they could freely choose a school, all they'd have to do is show up one morning with a child and tuition money, and the child would be enrolled.

The reality of most private schools is far different – they are highly selective. Private schools with excellent academic programs usually have stringent entrance requirements. Parents and students alike are interviewed in depth to insure a "good fit" between the family and the school. Parents are often "encouraged" to volunteer a significant amount of time on behalf of the school, in the event their child is granted admission.

For example, despite tuitions that range from almost $5,000 to over $10,000 per year, San Francisco's private high schools are deluged with applications for admission. Even without vouchers, applications at some of these exclusive schools are exceeding available spaces by four to one. Competition is so stiff that some parents hire consultants at $110 an hour to help with applications. In addition to student essays, parents have to write essays as well, describing their own children. Does this sound like parental choice to you?

Any choice involved in most private school admissions is made by the school, not by the parent. As with college enrollment, parents wait by the phone to see if their offspring is worthy of entry.

Public schools can't operate this way. If a child lives in a community supported by the school, admission is guaranteed. The parent's job status, prison record, religious beliefs, fluency in English, or other attributes providing evidence for a "good fit" are irrelevant. Public schools accept every child; evidence of the student's academic prowess – or lack thereof – is not relevant, unless the child needs the services of a special day school (also provided through public money). In other words, public schools are open to all.

Because private schools are selective (and will continue to be when vouchers are implemented), the voucher system becomes a method for circumventing equitable educational access guaranteed by Brown vs. Board of Education. Yes, most private schools are forbidden from discriminating on the basis of race, but subtle methods exist to insure that private schools select those students, and only those students, that they really want to have.

As for the children who are left behind... well, that is someone else's problem.

If parents want their children to attend private schools, that is fine. A problem arises when money is taken from public schools to help offset private school tuition. Because private schools will become even more selective if vouchers become a reality, the children remaining in public institutions will be those that the private schools don't want – children of poverty, children whose parents don't care about education, children who don't fit the image of Norman Rockwell's America. Furthermore, public school teachers will be dealing with more "at risk" children than ever before, and have fewer resources with which to meet the needs of these children. Experienced teachers will burn out sooner and will leave the system (this is already happening, by the way) and our public schools will be filled with needy children deprived of the resources needed to help them become full partners in the American dream while some children with the "right" credentials receive public subsidies for a private education in fantasy land – the prep school world of the upper class.

Vouchers are so antithetical to the concept of equal opportunity that I'm amazed that anyone would have the courage to publicly support such an obvious erosion of our democratic ideals.

Some claim that private schools provide better education than public schools. How valid is that argument?

No one will argue that private schools provide a different educational experience than public schools. Prayer services at the start of the school day can be an enriching experience for some children, and they are denied this opportunity in public schools. But if we look at the academic rigor of public vs. private schools, we are likely to find the same spread of quality in the K-12 range as we find in colleges. There are some public colleges and universities that are incredibly rigorous, and others that are party schools. Private colleges share the same qualities.

Many of the private schools that show incredible academic results are very selective in their admission policies. They look at the students – and at the parent's willingness to provide strong support for the child's academic development. While public school teachers universally attempt to engage parents in classroom activities, and encourage parents to provide all the support they can for their child's intellectual development, they are powerless to require this level of commitment.

Some private schools have support materials that most public school teachers would die for. Parents at some of these schools insure that the school has the latest computer equipment for the children, for example. On the other hand, some private schools are very poorly equipped. A few years ago I found a private school with science textbooks so old they wrote about a future when "man may one day walk on the moon."

Our public schools have done an excellent job in improving student success in school, even though (as we will explore later) there are many changes that need to be made in both private and public education to prepare students for life in the 21st century.

I think it fair to say that private schools, on the whole, are neither better nor worse than public schools. They provide a different experience, that's all.

Finally, let's look at the belief that competition will improve the quality of public schools.

The premise behind this argument is that public schools have no incentive to improve. One way to provide incentive is to create competition. Once public schools start losing money, it is argued, they will shape up.

Stanford University professor Terry Moe is a staunch defender of this argument. He claims that public schools are poorly run; that they are unwieldy bureaucracies prone to waste and fiscal mismanagement. Curiously, an article on this topic by Dr. Moe appeared in the Peninsula Times Tribune (a newspaper serving the San Francisco bay area) on January 5, 1992 – the same day that Stanford's mismanagement of government grant money was being described in some detail on the same page of the paper. I agree that mismanagement is an issue of concern, but this issue is as important for private schools like Stanford as it is for public schools.

The amazing thing about the argument that fiscal competition will improve public schools is that it is so illogical. For example, voucher proponents claim that, once schools start losing students and money, they will have the incentive to improve themselves. If this is such a wonderful idea, why doesn't industry try it? Imagine a corporate leader walking into a company R&D department and announcing: "Because of increased competition from abroad, we are going to reduce your budget to get you to work harder."

It is inconceivable that any responsible leader would ever make this statement, yet this is exactly what voucher proponents think will help our schools.

Of course voucher proponents don't want public schools to succeed. Many of them (including Channel One's Chris Whittle) think that public education is beyond repair. Mr. Whittle, a businessman from Knoxville, Tennessee, is investing $60 million in a three year project to design a new school. He will then invest $2.5 billion to construct 200 of these schools in anticipation of creating thousands of them throughout the country. These schools are designed to be a money-making operation, and Mr. Whittle is very clear on this point. If he had 4% of the market, his business would rake in $10 billion per year. Numbers like that make entrepreneurs drool.

But wouldn't it be nice if we had the guts to make this kind of investment in our public schools? I don't see anyone jumping at the chance to put $60 million into a three-year project to fix a single public school. The New American Schools Development Corporation will spread a small fraction of that amount (up to $3 million per school per year) over a dozen schools in five years. While efforts of this scale are to be applauded, they pale in comparison to the kind of investment Whittle and his supporters are willing to make in schools of their design.

The fact of the matter is that many of our schools are massively underfunded. By draining money from schools that need it most, we will accelerate the demise of public education, and speed the disenfranchisement of those students for whom education is the only path out of poverty.

Voucher systems allow parents to take "their" money and apply it to private school tuition, rather than working within the community to help public schools rebuild and change for the next century. This is the fastest way I know to turn America into a third world country.

Are there some schools so poorly managed that they fail to meet student needs? Yes. Are there educators who should find another line of work? Yes. Can we identify these problems by looking at standardized test scores out of context? No.

Universal access to quality public education is a cornerstone of our democracy. Schools are not part of the free-market any more than our soldiers are. If we rush to implement vouchers, what happens to those children whose special needs make them unlikely candidates for private school? What about the families who, even with their vouchers, will be unable to send their children to the school of their choice because they can't make up the tuition differential, lack the time required to bring the child to school, or can't take part in mandatory parent involvement at the school site?

We have a school system intended to meet the needs of a democratic nation. We are continuing to make steady progress in the face of constant criticism. Teachers continue to work in unsafe buildings for a fraction of what they could earn in private industry.

If, as many argue, we are failing to meet the needs of our children, we must work within the schools to change them for the better – otherwise we risk the destruction of public education by the end of the decade.

❄ Education for the 21st Century

Because the underlying premise of the old model educational institutions runs counter to the needs of students in the 21st century, we cannot achieve our goals by simply extending the school year, nor by creating new tests of achievement alone. We need to redefine the meaning of education in terms that meet the needs of the post-industrial age.

Technology has the power to help facilitate this change, but technology must be thought about in the context of meaningful restructuring of the educational process. The reason for this is that technology can be applied in education to meet many objectives. Technology is, by itself, neutral. The hammer with which Michelangelo created the Pieta can be used to destroy it. For this reason it is essential that we place pedagogy above technology and allow our focus on technological futures to be guided by core beliefs and understandings about our goals and our awareness of ways to develop and maintain a lifelong interest in education in all learners.

Societal Change and Education
The world is changing, and the rate of change is accelerating. Numerous authors have been writing about this topic for many years. But we no longer need to rely on the crystal balls of others to see changes in society. We can see evidence of this in changing employment patterns, the changing demographics of our communities, and in changes in the information technology found in our homes.

For example, consider the following graph of tax return information from the IRS:

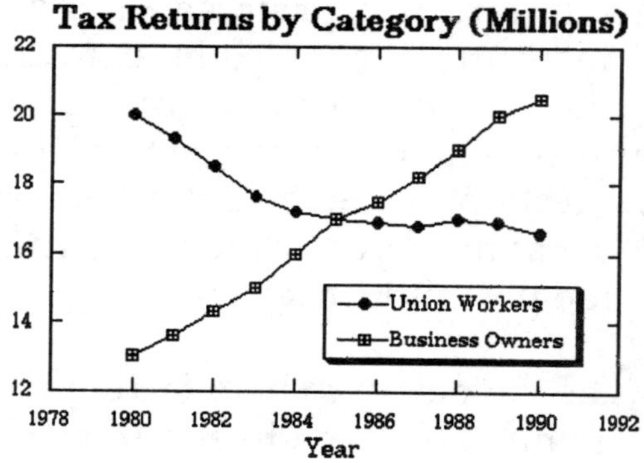

This graph shows the decline in the number of blue collar workers and the concomitant rise in owners of small businesses over the past 10 years. Add to this the fact that the skills needed by blue collar workers have changed in the past decade, and it is clear that our educational system needs to meet needs of a very different clientele than it had just a decade ago.

Census data show remarkable changes in our population in the past decade – especially in the Pacific Rim states. For example, the following chart shows the population changes for our most populous state – California. The increase in limited-English speaking peoples is reflected in the strong growth in Hispanic and Asian populations in the past decade. The changes reported in this chart are being felt elsewhere as well.

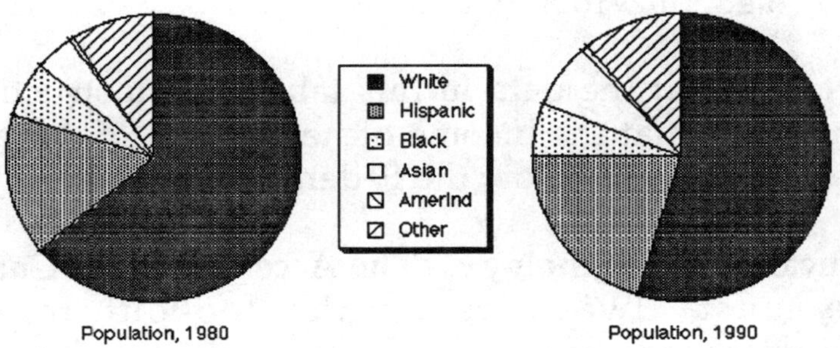

Technology and non-print literacy are commonplace in the life of our youth. The left-right, top-bottom world of Gutenberg has been joined by an explosion of non-linear and (in many cases) highly interactive information tools in the home. The following data from the Electronics Industries Association shows just how pervasive technology has become in our homes:

Technology	January 1991 Penetration (% of U.S. Households)
Telephone	99
Color Television	97
Component Audio	94
VCR	74
Cable	59
Computer	29
Audio CD Player	28
Projection Video	7

In looking at the data in this table, it is instructive to remember that the income of nearly 14% of American households falls below the Federal poverty levels.

Educational Technology – The Acceleration of Change

We must always be on the lookout for new technologies that can have a positive impact on education; but this presents us with an immediate challenge: How do we plan for the future when technology is advancing by leaps and bounds? Our answer to this question is that we first identify the solid curricular and pedagogical ideas that we believe in, and then equip our classrooms with the best technologies currently available to do this job, with the understanding that some of these technologies may be augmented or replaced in the years to come.

This much is clear: We need to stop investing in technologies of the past – we are beyond the age of 16mm movie projectors. *When you travel at the speed of light, you don't need a rear view mirror.*

❄ When I Was My Child's Age – Paradigm's Lost

Once a photograph of the Earth, taken from the outside, is available... a new idea as powerful as any in history will let loose.

Sir Fred Hoyle, 1948

So far I seem to be saying two things in this book. First, our educational system is doing a better job than ever in schooling our children. Second, we need to radically restructure education if it is to meet the needs of the next century. Are these two statements contradictory? I don't think so. The problem with our educational system is not that it has been doing its task badly – it is that the task of education has not changed to meet the needs of the time. As I said in the Introduction, schools are the only institution in our society that have remained fairly untouched by the advances of the past thirty years. Given the age and future needs of education's customers, schools should be leaders, not followers, in the pace of self-transformation.

To illustrate the need for this transformation, I'll tell a personal story: Two years or so ago my son, Harvey, and I were looking at the images of Neptune's moons being sent from the furthest reaches of our solar system. Harvey was a Junior in high school at the time, and was very interested in science (he still is). As the images flashed on the television screen during a news show, I said, "Harvey, isn't this the most fantastic thing you've ever seen?"

"Oh, dad," he said, "it's pretty good."

"Pretty good!" I replied. Where was the feeling of majesty, acknowledgment of the incredible nature of the feat?

Harvey said, "Well, dad, the signal is so small by the time it reaches Earth that they probably have to use very high bandwidths for noise reduction. They are probably using multiply-redundant transmissions for their error-correction algorithms, and the color data probably won't be here for another day or so."

I looked at Harvey as if he had stepped from a spaceship himself, and then he said something I will never forget: "Dad, you have to remember that there was never a time in my life when we weren't space explorers."

That hit like a ton of bricks. Of course he was right; but there was plenty of time in MY life when space travel was a dream. In fact, in 1956, when I was in school, British Astronomer Royal, Dr. Richard van der Riet Wooley said, "Space travel is utter bilge." And then, a few years later, we saw this:

The view of the Earth as seen from space signaled a major shift in our world-view. Those whose formative years (generally thought to be between birth and age 6) occurred before we explored space have a very different world-view or paradigm than those who were born afterwards. By 1969 we had placed a man on the moon, and returned him safely to Earth. The world changed.

I'm not suggesting that this one event was responsible for the paradigm shift all by itself, but it is symbolic of it. During the time of the "space race," nascent technologies became mature. The world of digital electronics and random-access devices grew at a phenomenal rate. The 60's marked a transition to an era some have never fully accepted.

The problem we now encounter in education is simply this: Our children operate with a completely different world-view than that of many adults. As educators, we have a sacred duty to support and enhance the development of our youth, not to try to convert them to outmoded ways of thinking. This, then, is the pivotal challenge of our time.

When I was my child's age...

Several years ago I was sitting in a fast-food restaurant by myself and, during lunch, I overheard a conversation between two couples at an adjacent table. One man said to another, "Today's kids have it too easy. They get driven to school; in my day I walked – four miles."

It seemed to me that this wasn't much of a story – after all, you need at least a ten-mile hike, barefoot, through the snow, uphill, both ways, to make a good tale. But before I could direct my attention elsewhere, he said, "... and I came home for lunch!"

Well, since we were now up to a 16 mile hike each day, I decided to stay tuned. What followed was the usual litany in defense of Readin', Ritin' and Rithmetic as being the only curriculum of value.

One of my Canadian friends, Gerry Morgan, has a great way to handle this argument when it is made by parents: "Will you ever be your child's age again?" he asks. Of course the answer is "No." But think about this: Will your child someday be your age now? The answer this time is "Yes."

What year will it be when your child is your age? You'll most likely get a year well into the next century – 2020, or beyond. What will life be like in 2020? We there be new jobs? Will we have cities on Mars? Will the world be markedly different from today?

To answer this last question, think about the year 1960 and look around your home or office. What kinds of information tools do you have today? Color TV with push-button remote control, VCR, cassette tape deck, CD player, personal computer – the list goes on. Look in your kitchen. What do you see there? Microwave oven, compact food processor? Go to the garage or car port. How many microprocessors does your car contain? How much of your automobile is made with new alloys and plastics?

And now – how much of this was available in 1960? None of it.

While technological changes have become obvious in the past 30 years, they are not the only transformations we have to deal with. The Red Menace has disappeared along with the Soviet Union. Trading groups are replacing political alliances. And the list goes on.

So here is the challenge we face when a parent talks about the "good old days." We can only do one thing at a time. Which would the parent wish: that we prepare children for the parent's past, or for their child's future? Put in this context, the answer is obvious – we must prepare people for their future, not for our past.

Intransigent parents are not the sole cause of the problem. We all resist change. We are defined by our paradigms, and feel assaulted when they are threatened. Even futurists are caught with their paradigms down, as I was when Harvey reminded me about the world in which he grew up.

Fr. Stanley Bezuska at Boston College has collected examples of resistance to change in education spanning the last 200 years or so. His collection of quotations will probably bring a smile to your face, so here they are:

Students today can't prepare bark to calculate their problems. They depend on their slates which are more expensive. What will they do when the slate is dropped and it breaks? They will be unable to write! (Teacher's Conference, 1703)

Students today depend on paper too much. They don't know how to write on a slate without getting chalk dust all over themselves. They can't clean a slate properly. What will they do when they run out of paper?

(Principal's Association, 1815)

Students today depend too much upon ink. They don't know how to use a pen knife to sharpen a pencil. Pen and ink will never replace the pencil.
(National Association of Teachers, 1907)

Students today depend upon store bought ink. They don't know how to make their own. When they run out of ink they will be unable to write words or ciphers until their next trip to the settlement. This is a sad commentary on modern education.
(The Rural American Teacher, 1928)

Students today depend on these expensive fountain pens. They can no longer write with a straight pen and nib. We parents must not allow them to wallow in such luxury to the detriment of learning how to cope in the real business world which is not so extravagant.
(PTA Gazette, 1941)

Ballpoint pens will be the ruin of education in our country. Students use these devices and then throw them away. The American values of thrift and frugality are being discarded. Business and banks will never allow such expensive luxuries.
(Federal Teachers, 1950)

Students today depend too much on hand-held calculators...
(?, 1992)

If you are like most people who've seen this list, you

probably smiled until you read the last one. Suddenly the paradigm shift hits the fan! We find it amusing to look at how quaint some of the other concerns were, totally forgetting that, a few years from now, educators will view our reluctance to let children use calculators in the same way we now view those who refused to let them use paper (instead of slates).

The point, for now, anyway, is that educators are not immune from getting stuck in outmoded world-views, and they never were.

The nature of paradigms

We all experience the same world, but we see it through glasses colored by our dominant world-views. As Marcel Proust once said, "The real act of discovery consists not in finding new lands but in seeing with new eyes."

None of us is immune from paradigm myopia. As educators, though, we have a special need to overcome it. The world of our children is so different from that of our parents that we and our educational institutions need to change if we expect our system of formal education to be relevant in the lives of our youth.

Try this experiment the next time you visit your home town (assuming you've been gone for a decade or so). Walk down the main street and make a list of all the changes you can find. That automated teller machine on the corner – was that there before? The video rental store – what did that used to be? How about the supermarket? Where is the long pole with the package grippers on the end to bring items down from the tall shelves? Where did that bar code reader come from? The corner hardware store that used to have oak cabinets holding loose screws now has neatly packaged assortments hanging from a wire rack.

I made this trip down memory lane in my home town earlier this year. Virtually everything had changed – except the schools. The buildings were the same, the halls smelled the same, the rooms looked pretty much the same (the desks now move, and the blackboards are now green). In other words, not much has changed physically in many of our schools.

What about uses of technology? When I was in school we were not allowed to use pocket calculators under any circumstances. Of course that was because they hadn't been invented yet. But even today, with good basic calculators available at the corner drugstore for under $3, many teachers still refuse to allow universal access to these tools. Instead, they persist in teaching children to "divide, multiply, subtract, bring down" for long division, just as they did in my day.

I once offered a prize to anyone who could name a 21st century occupation in which workers would not have universal access to calculators whenever they needed them. After making this offer to 17,000 people through my workshops, I finally found one winner. What occupation still does not guarantee access to a calculator to any professional who needs it? Fourth-grade teacher.

While we hang onto our hallowed paradigms, crafting clever defenses for the status quo, our children continue to speed away from us and the educational system we have saddled them with.

Some parents are well-educated and rich enough to insure that their children have access to today's information tools at home. Others are not so fortunate. As a result, we run the very real risk that the gap between the financially rich and poor will turn into a gap between the informationally rich and poor. This will result in complete disenfranchisement of a large part of our population and could cripple our country.

How to we dig ourselves out of this mess?

Money is not the answer, although it will be part of the solution. We spend a lot of money on education already (although, world-wide, our expenditures are in line with other major countries.) The problem is that we seem to be investing our money in reinforcement of the prevailing, yet outdated, paradigm. We seem to be asking the wrong questions.

All too often we use money to replace outdated materials, rather than wonder if these materials should take a new form altogether. For example, virtually every classroom in America today has a wall map for which a significant portion of the land mass is improperly labeled. There is no USSR anymore, and we should remove these maps immediately, unless we are teaching history. But with what should we replace these maps? This question doesn't get asked at most schools. Old wall maps are replaced with new wall maps, and the cycle continues.

There is another path. Suppose we ask this question: *Given the technologies that exist today, what tools should we make available to all students to let them explore the geography and political boundaries of the natural satellites of the Solar system?*

This question acknowledges that, in addition to the Earth, we have fairly accurate information on the geographical features of close to 40 natural satellites. It also acknowledges that a static wall map may not be the best choice today.

My guess is that fewer than 1% of our school districts will even ask this question, let alone respond to it. We are likely to continue mistaking the edge of the rut for the horizon.

This phenomenon is called "paradigm paralysis" by Joel Barker, author of *Future Edge: Discovering the New Paradigms of Success*. Joel's focus is on industry, since corporate America gets caught by change almost as much as education. He illustrates this in several ways, one of which I found quite interesting.

IBM has been in the computer business for a long time. As a dominant player, IBM defined the business. Basically, by 1977, the established paradigm was this:

- IBM made its own chips
- IBM wrote its own software
- IBM had a captive sales force
- IBM computers were sealed – you couldn't add your own devices

In the same year, Apple computer entered the market with a new paradigm defined by the Apple II:

- Apple bought its chips from the outside
- Apple relied on outside software vendors
- Apple sold its computers through retail channels
- Apple provided slots for users to add their own devices

The amazing thing was that, by the time IBM introduced its own personal computer in 1982, they had adopted Apple's paradigm entirely. Was this painful for IBM? I'm sure it was. Was this strategy successful? Look at the desktops in many large corporations and you'll see the answer yourself.

The world does not stand still. Apple introduced the Macintosh in 1984, and with it an even newer paradigm to the general public – that of the graphical user interface. At the time of introduction, the Mac was viewed as a toy by those who saw computing as a serious number-crunching endeavor. What these critics missed is that, even though the early Macintosh was underpowered for many tasks, it defined a new benchmark for the industry.

What is the hot software for non-Apple computers today? Windows. What does it do? It allows users of IBM-compatible computers to have some of the ease of use that Macintosh owners have had since the mid-80's. Once again, the bar has been raised, the paradigm has shifted, and industries have had to respond or die.

How often do we make similar kinds of changes in education? Change in education comes slowly, if at all. There are many reasons for this. First, unlike corporations, educational institutions have to prepare people for their entire lives. This implies that changes, when made, must be made with caution. On the other hand, our educational institutions – from Kindergarten through college – have many managers, and few leaders. As Barker says in his book, managers manage within the context of a prevailing paradigm. Leaders take us from one paradigm to another.

One of the buzzwords in education today is site-based management. I suggest that what we need instead is site-based leadership. These leaders – and I count all educators among their potential ranks – must know how to think intelligently about the future. The reason for this is expressed eloquently by Barker: "It is in the future where our greatest leverage is. We can't change the past, although, if we are smart, we learn from it. Things happen in only one place – the present. And usually we react to those events. The "space" of time in the present is too slim to allow for much more. It is in the yet-to-be, the future, and only there, where we have the time to prepare for the present."

And it is to this future time that we now shift our focus.

❄ Present Tense and Future Perfect

If you agree that educators need to be futurists, the next logical question might be: How does one learn to think intelligently about the future?

There are many well-known futurists, and even more who do very good work hidden from public view. What I hope to show in this chapter is that you can become an expert at predicting (and creating) the future for your classroom, school or district.

The method we will use is one well-known to many futurists, John Naisbitt, Faith Popcorn, Alvin Toffler, Marvin Cetron, Joel Barker and Stanley Davis, to name just a few. It is called trend analysis. When we read books like Naisbitt's *Megatrends*, or *Megatrends 2000*, we are looking at the future through one set of lenses. When we read Toffler's *Powershift*, or Popcorn's *Popcorn Report*, we see other sets of trends, many overlapping with those of other authors.

Because the popular authors primarily focus on societal and business trends, education does not receive as much attention as it might. Later on, I'll share some trends I see in education, but more importantly, you should be on the lookout for new trends yourself.

The problem with forecasts...

Before embarking on the process of trend identification, you need to know why this process has a chance of working. In re-reading the great dystopian and utopian novels (e.g., Thomas More's *Utopia*, Bellamy's *Looking Backwards*, Huxley's *Brave New World*, Orwell's *1984*) I was struck by two observations. In all cases the authors overestimated the rate of societal change and underestimated the rate of technological change. The only author who comes even close in technology forecasting is Jules Verne. When recently asked about the technology depicted in the science fiction classic, *2001*, the book's author, Arthur C. Clarke, spoke for many of us when he said, "The future isn't what it used to be."

From our perspective, these observations tell us two things. First, as far as education is concerned, any technology you can conceive will probably be available, inexpensively, in very few years. Do you want a full color video projector you can carry in a coat pocket? It is on the market today. Do you want students to be able to step inside environments modeling different gravitational systems? Virtual reality lets you do this. Do you want to scrap your flat television images in favor of 3-D images constructed in front of the viewer's eyes? It is happening in video game arcades now. Would you like students to be able to hum a melody and have it transcribed in musical notation on the computer screen? This, too, is available today. In the world of technology, Walt Disney's message rings true: "If you can dream it, you can do it."

Don't be hampered by the past. Don't think in terms of last week's technologies. When you are traveling at the speed of light, you don't need a rearview mirror.

In the area of societal change, things move more slowly. This means that there are some long-term trends that will probably continue to shape our lives into the next century. If we can identify these trends, then, coupled with the extremely rapid pace of technological change, we will have the tools with which to design the future of education.

Present tense

One of the more popular routes taken in the restructuring process involves assessing where our institutions are today, projecting where they should be, and then preparing a plan to allow us to catch up. For example, imagine that society (educators, students, parents, business leaders, and the general public) has one view of where education should be in terms of the physical plant, pedagogical models, technology, curriculum, time in school, etc. Of course, in reality, there won't be any one agreed-upon assessment of education's needs, but let's pretend for the moment that there is. Now, let's assume that, after careful evaluation, you conclude that your schools are functioning at a level from the past. The temptation is to think that the key to improvement is a plan that lets you "catch up."

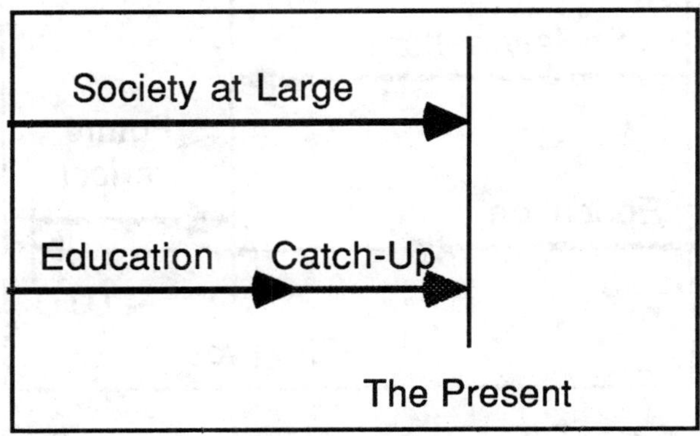

This is the dominant paradigm for restructuring – and it is almost guaranteed to fail. Here's why. Suppose you make a list of curricular and technological reforms based on the latest information available and decide to restructure around these tools and ideas. By the time your plan is implemented, the present will have become the past and you will once again find yourself out of date. This is one of the reasons why I'm not concerned about schools preparing students for Workforce 2000. If we changed everything today, we'd still only impact about 20% of the people who will be working at the turn of the century.

If the catch-up game doesn't work (and I am convinced that it can't) then what is the alternative? According to Stanley Davis, author of *Future Perfect*, we need to skip past the present to a date well into the future, design a system that makes sense for that time, and then make changes now that fit with a longer-term view. In this manner we then speak of the future as if it had already happened – the future perfect tense.

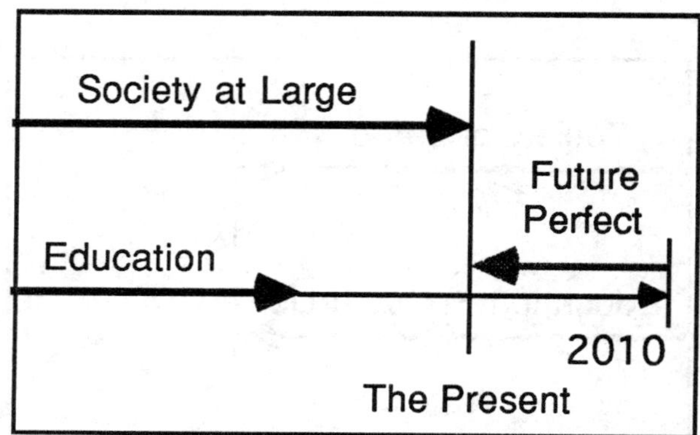

Now there are a few details that have to be worked out. For example, which year should you choose for your forecast? And how, in the face of rapid change, do you plan for a time well into the next century?

These are excellent questions, and they have answers. The year I've chosen for consideration in this book is 2010. I've chosen this year for two reasons. First, we have time to implement some new ideas before students from the graduating class of 2010 enter our schools. Second, while technologies are going to undergo revolutionary changes in the coming years, there are probably a few issues that will remain as compelling in 2010 as they are today; or, if they have changed, they will change slowly enough for us to track them and make adjustments on the way.

To explore the validity of this latter argument, look back 30 years to 1962. We had yet to place a man on the moon, we perceived the Soviet Bloc as an aggressor, and the label Made in Japan was synonymous with "junk." Yet, to the careful observer, signs of change were visible – even then. The roller coaster of the past few years is running on a track whose design was perceptible 30 years ago. While the apparent pace of transformation seems to be faster than it once was, we are still likely to be able to identify some of the major influences that will shape education's needs for the next two decades.

Trend finding

These influences, or trends, can be found several ways. One good starting point is to read as many books on the future as you can. Many of these books are well written, and are the result of an incredible amount of research. When you finish your reading, make a list of those areas where the authors seem to be in agreement. You'll be surprised at the agreement you'll find. While it is possible for many highly paid experts to all make the same mistake, their collective insights are still worth exploring.

But don't rely completely on outsiders. First, very few futurists are devoting their efforts entirely to education. To my knowledge, this book is, at its time of publication, the only one of its kind on the market. This means that you have to do your own research, check out your own hunches, and build a clippings file to keep track of ideas that may emerge into trends.

Where do you go trend hunting? Lots of places. First, in the technology domain, make it a monthly practice to walk the electronics aisles of Toys "R" Us, or some other toy megastore. Visit electronics "superstores" to see the latest in home entertainment and home video equipment. If possible, treat yourself to one of the two Consumer Electronics shows in Las Vegas (January) or Chicago (May or June) to see what is coming next. Read as many technology magazines as you can, looking for articles on future trends, and scanning the ads for new technologies.

In the area of education, keep up with Education Week and other journals, and attend as many conferences as you can. If you can't get to the conferences, order tape recordings of the major speeches.

Make good use of on-line information services once you've identified topics to explore in more depth, or subscribe to the Magazine Rack CD-ROM which contains the full text of 300 professional and popular magazines in a wide spectrum of subject areas. I'll often sit down with a current version of this disc, type in a few key words, and then go fishing until I hit something I'd never find if I was scanning magazines by eye.

What are you looking for? Keep your eyes on the renegades and crackpots. Established companies and many full professors are in the "evolution" business. You want to see the revolutionary ideas that can lead to new paradigms. Try to identify the paradigm pioneers and see if their ideas can be transformed into something that makes sense to you. Remember, less than 20 years ago Apple Computer's Steve Jobs and Steve Wozniak were perceived as crackpots by the giant computer manufacturers, RCA, Control Data, Data General and others. (If you haven't a clue as to who these former "computer giants" are, the point is made.)

In the remainder of this book I'm going to illustrate the process of trend analysis and its application to designing schools for 2010. The trends I've chosen might not seem right to you. If so, please replace them with your own. It is the process, not the content, that is the most important.

That said, I currently believe that the following educational trends (Edutrends) will be applicable from now and to the year 2010 and beyond. These trends include:

- Change/Obsolescence
- Global Village
- National Educational Focus
- Educational Technology: Faster, Cheaper, Smaller
- Technomerge
- Choices/Learning Styles
- Egonomics/Constructivism

These trends come from several sources. Some I found on my own, others in discussion with other futurists, and some from popular books on the topic. To understand my thinking behind the choice of these trends, let's explore them one at a time.

Change/Obsolescence

Early in 1992 it was reported that the President of Rand McNally sent a memo to his managers informing them that countries had until July 1 to change their borders if they expected to get into the new atlas. This phenomenon (which I jokingly call "Rand McNally psychosis") is an attempt to deal with rates of change unknown to our generation. The world is literally changing. Rather than this being the typical "end of the century" phenomenon I described in the introduction, I think we are in for a sustained period of rapid change lasting decades. For some perspective on this viewpoint, you should read Lynch and Kordis' *Strategy of the Dolphins.*

In addition to changes in the political world, we are seeing reversals and flip flops in other parts of society. Religious leaders in the 60's went to jail protesting for civil rights, or an end to the war in Vietnam. Today some of them are going to jail for raiding the church coffers.

We are being told to change our educational system to be more like that of the Japanese, and they are in the process of shortening their school year to make their system look more like ours.

When we were in school, teachers had to deal with talking in class and tardiness. Today teachers are dealing with drugs and guns.

Whether the pace of change has truly increased, or we are just more aware of change than ever before, we still must respond. The half-life of scientific information is now about 5 years, and is expected to drop to 2 years by the end of the century. One question that this brings to mind is: *What is the value of a textbook that results from a 4 year adoption process in a world where half the information in that book might be obsolete the day it is opened by a student for the first time?*

Global Village

One of the stranger battles in the War of 1812 (immortalized in song) was the Battle of New Orleans. As you may recall from the song, this "little trip" started in 1814 as Jackson moved his troops south to engage the British. The battle itself took place in January of 1815, weeks after the war was officially ended by the signing of the Treaty of Ghent on Christmas Day, 1814. Information delivery was so slow that many lives were lost fighting a battle that took place after the war was over.

Contrast this with our 1991 engagement with Iraq in which CNN showed us events *as they were happening*. This was truly the "CNN War" as my friend Ian Jukes calls it. Each of us can think of numerous times, in the past year, when the news we heard in the morning was completely different from the news we heard in the evening. Changes, anywhere on the globe, are instantly available to us anywhere and anytime we want them. A result of our communication tools is the apparent shrinking of the world. We don't think of global events as taking place in some remote "over there" to be picked out on a globe when we get the chance. Instead, these events are played out in our living rooms, bringing the world into our laps.

This speed and completeness of coverage gives us a chance to share areas of common concern. If our informational tools have "shrunk" the world, they have heightened our ability to be informed about the status of this blue ball we call home. In watching international telecommunication projects linking children all over the world, I am impressed with the deep concern our children have for the environment. The "green" movement has grown from regional activism to a global movement, with children at the cutting edge. I expect this level of concern to remain the same, or perhaps even grow, in the coming years.

The challenge this places on schools is quite interesting. All too often our classrooms are set up according to the "2 x 4 x 6" rule: They are defined by the two covers of a book, the four walls of a classroom, and six periods a day. There is still some value in providing places for quiet repose, isolated from the hustle and bustle of reality, but I seriously question whether these places should be called schools. One question this brings to mind is: *In this age of global transformation, does it make sense to have classrooms without telephones, modems and TV cables with which teachers and students can connect to the outside world?*

National Educational Focus

As we've explored in previous chapters, the public is increasingly concerned about the state of education in this country. I don't expect this interest to wane. In fact, this is an international phenomenon. An article by Mary Jordan in the March 29, 1992 Washington Post describes the pressure being placed on Japanese educators to *reduce* the school year. Osami Shima, spokesman for the Japan Teacher's Union in Tokyo, says that the current Japanese system stifles student creativity and the spirit of individualism. Japan expects to trim its school year significantly in response to pressures to meet the needs of today's Japanese citizen.

We, of course, are being pressured in the opposite direction, but that is not the point here. The relevant point is that schools throughout the world are receiving and, in some cases, responding to pressures that come from outside the system.

Parents have always wanted schools to "do the right thing;" what is different today is the level of vocal activism that surrounds education. A question this raises is this: *What can schools do to help forge effective collaborations with the community to insure that our society is properly served by our educational system?*

Educational Technology: Faster, Cheaper, Smaller

We'll have a lot to say on this topic in a few chapters, but for now I'll just belabor the obvious. Computer technology that required a complete room in 1960 could be placed on a desk 10 years ago, can be placed on your lap today, and will fit in your shirt pocket by the end of 1992. That's not a brave prediction, that's just what you see walking down the aisles of any technology trade show. The really interesting questions have to do with access: *Is it appropriate to deny technology to any child when there is hardly a single career in his/her lifetime that will not require the effective use of informational tools?*

Technomerge

As with the previous trend, this one will be explored in depth later. As explained by Ian Jukes and Ted McCain (who call the phenomenon "technological fusion"), the idea behind Technomerge is that, with time, our electronic information devices are merging into one box. In the late 70's, computer users had their equipment connected to a monitor and printer, and that was about it. Today's multimedia station consists of a computer plugged into a wide range of devices including CD-ROM drives, laser videodiscs, and other gadgetry – each with its own cable. Student workstations today are looking more and more like a rat's nest of cables as our technologies become more integrated in their functionality.

In 1991, Commodore released CDTV – an "information appliance" that connects to a television and uses a hand-held remote control similar to that used with VCR's and other home entertainment products. Unlike other products, CDTV is a complete Amiga computer system with a built-in CD-ROM disc drive. Everything is packaged in one sleek box that looks more at home among stereo equipment than on a computer desk. More importantly, this device is so easy to use that the instruction manual is only six pages long. Similar devices (such as the CD-I system from Phillips) indicate a trend toward the integration of technologies (Technomerge) and increased simplicity of use. We expect this trend to start slowly, but gather steam in the coming years.

One of the challenges of these information appliances is getting the public to buy them. Unless these products become commercial successes, they will never have an impact on education – the market is just too small to support these technologies. Phillips, however, is betting very strongly on the success of CD-I. I think one of the reasons that Phillips bought 15% of Blockbuster video stores was to guarantee rack space for the CD-I titles. Software sells hardware.

This trend raises a question: *What will student reports look like when every child has access to multimedia workstations?*

Choices/Learning Styles

Henry Ford once said of his cars, "You can have any color you want, so long as it's black." In the early days of industry, uniformity and mass production went hand in hand. As production techniques advanced, the public found that it could demand, and receive, customized products at mass produced prices. Today's fast food phrase, "We'll make it your way," has replaced the uniformity of the old industrial order.

When Horace Mann contributed to the design of public schools in the 1800's, his model was the old industrial system that focussed on uniformity of experience rather than on individualization of instruction. The educational system of the 19th (and most of the 20th) century kept time a constant, and allowed learning to be the variable. This is changing now that educators and educational leaders are realizing that our system can – and must – accommodate the needs of different learners.

Many modern pedagogies are based on the idea that

learning pathways can be different for each child, even if the student/teacher ratio is 30 to 1. Harvard University's Howard Gardner has formulated a theory of multiple intelligences that has been applied to education by Thomas Armstrong and others as a way for classroom teachers to help each student learn in his/her own way. Bernice McCarthy's 4-MAT process (described in a later chapter) provides similar benefits through a different model. Add to these several other models that acknowledge the uniqueness of each learner, and it is clear that educational systems are responding to the Choices trend by accommodating individual learning styles.

While this movement took awhile to catch on, we see it having long term impact on education. One question that this trend raises is: *What will supplant the lecture as the other methods of instruction are developed?*

Egonomics/Constructivism

The term "egonomics" was coined by the futurist, Faith Popcorn to describe her observation that people were tending (or, we might say trending) toward the acquisition of things that provide them with personal comfort or a sense of personal accomplishment. This trend may be an outgrowth of the perceived facelessness of late 20th century work life, especially in large corporations. People are working harder than ever before, it seems, and now they want to take some personal joy in their labors.

In education, I see a similar trend in the move away from worksheets and toward a personally nurturing literature-based language arts curriculum, for example. Many educators are changing assessment methods, looking more for in-depth projects designed by students, than toward standardized tests.

The curriculum frameworks of several states (and British Columbia in Canada) are stressing the importance of performance-based assessment. These same documents also call for less emphasis on context-free skills development, and for more in-depth long-term projects. It is no longer enough that students memorize information; they are now expected to create artifacts (reports, projects, etc.) that demonstrate their understanding of the subject, and to express this understanding in unique ways.

A question this trend brings to mind is: *How long will it be before worksheets and multiple choice tests are banned from schools?*

What's next?

As I said earlier in this chapter, these trends are a few I think have long-term impact and utility for educators. You are encouraged to find more on your own, and to discard any of the ones I've listed if they don't make sense to you.

In the next few chapters we'll explore ideas behind some of the technology trends in more depth.

❄ The Death of Textbooks

A factor driving the curriculum in this country is the textbook – a compendium of piecemeal information written by a committee and edited in such a way as to offend no one. Most textbooks are so dreadfully written that the only reason anyone would be caught dead looking at one is because a teacher requires it. I'm continually amazed at the capacity of textbooks to take exciting topics and render them so empty of wonder and meaning that no one in his right mind could develop an interest in the subject from exposure to the textbook itself.

Looking at paradigms of educational change for the next century, I can safely predict the death of the textbook. Please note I'm not predicting the death of books – literature will (and should) continue to be published in printed form. The aesthetic experience of reading a good book cannot, yet, be replicated for most of us through technology. But textbooks don't even try to engage the reader. My generation used textbooks to hide the comic books we read in class; at least the comics told a story.

There is one feature of textbooks. They are repositories of information and they occasionally provide impetus to explore a subject in more depth. These functions can be performed much more easily by CD-ROM's. There are many reasons for thinking that the CD-ROM will displace the textbook in the near future (and at least one reason why it may not).

Reasons for ROM's

A 12 cm CD-ROM has the capacity to store about 275,000 pages of text. Some of this space can be traded off for other information – pictures, sounds, video clips, etc. But no matter how you look at it, the capacity of CD-ROM's is phenomenal.

Using 275,000 pages as a guide, how do books and CD-ROM's compare? On the basis of manufacturing cost, a 275,000 page library costs about $500 to print. The manufacturing cost of a CD-ROM is only $1.50. But then you'd have to ship the 275,000 page library (about 2750 pounds), compared to only 4 oz. for a CD-ROM in a plastic box.

In terms of impact on the environment, your 275,000 page library would consume about 23 trees, yet the CD-ROM uses only 16 grams of polycarbonate and a milligram or so of aluminum.

Even with high speed presses, it would take about 15 hours to print 275,000 pages, while the same amount of data could be pressed into a CD-ROM in 6 seconds. In other words, from the standpoint of economy and ecology, the CD-ROM wins hands-down, even if only a fraction of the disc space is used.

But there are other benefits that come from using CD-ROM's instead of books for course material. Some of these are listed below:

- Access speed: Any information stored on a CD-ROM can be retrieved in a few seconds (assuming the disc as been indexed). This index may occupy half the disc space or more, but is well worth the effort to create. The benefit of this index, of course, is that it can list every word – not just the ones a professional indexer thinks you might want to look up. How many times have you tried to find something in the index of a book only to discover that the word you are looking for was not deemed important enough to index? This happens to me all the time.

- Content variety: Books are well-suited for textual and pictorial information. CD-ROM's hold this type of information as well, along with sound files, film clips, animations and computer programs that model aspects of the subject being taught. Given our current interest in teaching in ways that honor individual learning styles, the textbook is an anachronism.

- Multiple pathways: Books are designed to be read from left to right, top to bottom. This Gutenbergian metaphor is forced by the

> medium. While this same metaphor can be (and, tragically, often is) incorporated in CD-ROM's, it need not be. CD-ROM databases can contain raw information with which the user can construct his or her own knowledge pathways.

As just one example of the kind of information that is being made available, NASA has released a 12-CD-ROM set of unedited images from the Voyager excursion to the outer planets. These discs (available as a set for under $100) can be used as image libraries in numerous ways. For example, some people will use the images as clip art for incorporation into written reports. Others will perform detailed analyses of the images, looking at the surface textures of the planets, for example. Still others will use these images as backdrops for interactive multimedia presentations – the list is endless. If your interest lies closer to home, similar sets of discs are available for the Viking mission (Mars), and the Magellan mission (Venus).

In the world of literature, World Library, Inc. has released its second edition of the Library of the Future. This one disc has the complete text and illustrations from 950 works of classical, cultural and historical literature. Two works can be displayed side-by-side for comparison, and text can be selected and saved to the user's disks for use in reports.

The sheer volume of information available in the CD-ROM format is beyond easy comprehension. Rather than constrain the placement and use of text or pictures, CD-ROM-based learning resources can be repurposed by students in ways that empower them to make meaning out of raw information. If the electronic medium did nothing else but this, it would be worth pursuing.

What's the catch?

Well, for one thing, CD-ROM drives have yet to become standard equipment on all computers. Even Apple – the first company to put a CD-ROM drive into the marketplace – has yet to realize that, by not building this drive into every computer they ship, they are as out of date as bell-bottom pants and 8-track audio tape decks. Some MS-DOS computer makers (Tandy, Magnavox, and others) have CD-ROM drives in some of their systems as they come out the door.

This much is clear: just as floppy disk drives became essential built-in devices in the 80's, built-in CD-ROM drives are essential in the 90's for any computer company who wants to meet the needs of education.

Sony is sneaking hardware into the classroom with CD-ROM's hidden in student book bags. The Data Discman is a pocket-sized CD-ROM player with a display screen and keyboard. The user places discs (containing, for example, the complete Compton's Encylopedia) into the player, types in a key word or phrase and, a few seconds later, the articles containing the desired information appear on the screen. Some teachers have called to ask me when they should do now that some of their kids have complete encyclopedias at their desk. Unlike pocket-sized dedicated encyclopedias, the Data Discman has a wide variety of software available for it including the complete works of Shakespeare, foreign language dictionaries, and numerous other reference works.

If Sony can make money when the Data Discman retails (with 3 reference works) for about $450, then there is no legitimate reason for any personal computer not to have a CD-ROM drive.

But, even if CD-ROM drives were free, and every child had one, another force would impede their use in education. First, textbook publishers are among the most conservative lot I've ever encountered. I half expect to see visor-clad scriveners poised over manuscripts with quills whenever I visit these folks. Many publishers see themselves in the book, rather than the information dissemination, business. As long as this remains the case, we will continue to see more print-based textbooks, and these will continue to be adopted by school districts and states whose curriculum advisors suffer from paradigm paralysis.

A blast from the past...

How do we blast these folks into the 20th century while there is still some of it left? This is a question we must address.

The reason this question is so important is because our children already live in the new paradigm – they are comfortable with electronic information retrieval. They spend hours glued to electronic devices of all sorts and, unless we do something drastic to push educational technology's horse-drawn carriage out of its 19th century quagmire, our kids will scoot past us in their electronic tin lizzies, sailing happily into a future in which todays classrooms have simply become irrelevant to learning.

Disktop Publishing

If textbooks will be replaced by electronic counterparts, will similar changes take place in the area of student-generated reports?

If you are like me, you probably remember handing in handwritten assignments. Throughout my entire schooling almost every single report, theme, or research project was submitted on paper.

Today, many students are submitting reports created with word processors. The graphic images in these reports are often created free-hand on the computer, or are chosen from a clip art library. Those who lack drawing skill are increasingly taking advantage of low-cost hand-held scanners that allow images to be snagged from a variety of sources to liven up their documents and illustrate important points. Once the document has been created in the computer, it is then printed out and handed in, just like the handwritten reports we wrote thirty years ago.

We are comfortable with this use of technology – so comfortable that we don't realize what we have done. Using computers to create reports that are printed on paper for submission is a lot like using a robot assembly line to manufacture buggy whips. We are using advanced technology to do things we did with old technology, without thinking about whether today's paper report has any relevance in the world of electronic information access.

We could save a lot of time and paper by submitting reports on disk. To start with, most printed information is sitting in a disk file already. The quantity of student-generated information that can be stored on one disk is huge. For example, the contents of a 400 page book can be stored, easily, on a single 3.5″ high density (1.44 megabyte) floppy disk. Disk copying, in small quantities, is quite inexpensive. A labeled disk with the content of a 400 page book costs about one dollar to manufacture. If you want to distribute a report to several people (or publish it, for that matter), you already have all the tools you need at your fingertips. Because disks can be duplicated using the same computer used to create the document in the first place, copies can be run off as they are needed.

But there is another advantage of disk-based information delivery: It allows us to move beyond the left-right, top-down world of Gutenberg. Written reports and books are intrinsically linear media; this need not be the case for computer-based materials. Take, for example, documents created in MediaText – a multimedia authoring environment designed by Professor Elliot Solloway and his colleagues at the University of Michigan (and distributed by Wings). This authoring tool looks a lot like a word processor, making it comfortable to those who are easing their way into electronic information distribution. Unlike documents destined for print, MediaText documents can include sound files, animations and other features that can't be placed on a printed page.

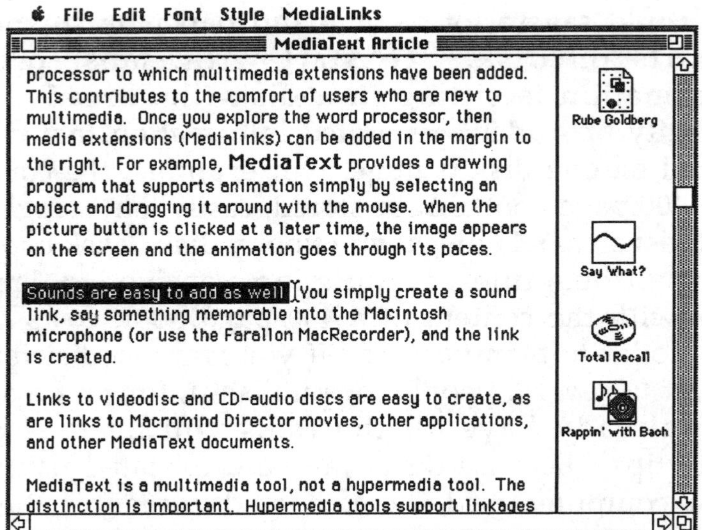

When you start MediaText, you will think you are using a simple Macintosh word processor with control over fonts, sizes, styles, etc. It is in the right margin where all the action takes place. This "media margin" is home for user-created buttons that bring up animated images, access frames or sequences on a videodisc, play sound files, play passages from audio CD's, launch other applications, or jump to other MediaText documents. MediaText will soon be able to play Apple's QuickTime videos.

The underlying idea behind MediaText was the same as that behind Kodak's Brownie camera – "You push the button, we do the rest." Just as the Brownie was used more for taking snapshots than for creating fine art photographs, MediaText is designed to bring multimedia authoring to the masses. Not everyone wants (or needs) to make the investment required to be a HyperCard expert.

For example, to create an animated sequence, you create a scene using the built-in object-based graphics program, choose the object you wish to animate, and drag it around the desired pathway with your mouse. The computer records this path and, the next time the picture is opened, any objects that have been animated will move through the paths you defined.

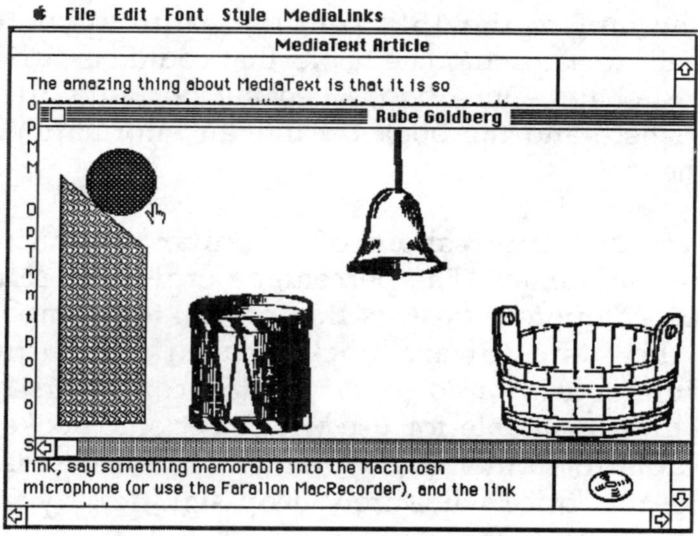

The beauty of this product is that MediaText is intuitively easy to learn, and the user can distribute completed documents on disk for others to play. Wings allows schools to send working copies of the software home, and Solloway has developed a royalty-free run-time version for those who want to send completed multimedia applications to others.

The challenge:
Printed books and reports still have one major

advantage over their disk-based counterparts: they require no extra hardware to render them readable. At present, user-created disk-based reports require access to a personal computer which, more likely than not, resides on a desk, not in the user's pocket. In this regard electronic books share the status of printed books before the time of Aldus Manutius. Old books were quite large and reading was a "desktop" activity. At the end of the 15th century Aldus invented a typeface to accommodate books that could be carried in a saddlebag. Once books became portable, literacy flourished, and the book became an information tool for the masses.

We are at the threshold of a similar revolution in electronic media. The percentage growth in sales of laptop computers exceeds that of desktop computers, and the trend toward pocket-based computing is continuing at a rapid pace. Laptop computers (with disk drives suitable for use with electronic books) are available for under $1,000, and, with history as our guide, this price will surely drop significantly in the coming years.

Disktop (as opposed to desktop) publishing offers three advantages over the publication of printed documents: lower cost, increased flexibility of information access, and ease of recycling for magnetic media. The disadvantages are cost and portability of the delivery platform. Given continuing advances in low-cost portable computers, these disadvantages will disappear in the coming years.

❄ Technomerge

Roger Wagner (the creator of HyperStudio) has described the VCR as the printer of the 90's. During a recent conversation, we discussed this issue at some length because of my interest in CD-ROM publishing and in the whole world of multimedia in general. I've suggested, over the years, that our communications media are merging in the sense that print-based information is now being supplemented by video and computer programs. According to my friend, Ian Jukes, this may be an intermediary phase to a completely integrated future.

Trend Watching

Ian quotes the work of British Columbia educational consultant and futurist, Ted McCain, who sees technological fusion taking place in stages. In 1967, for example, the worlds of computers, publishing, telecommunications and television did not overlap at all. Computers were number-crunching devices, and the text editors that existed at that time served the needs of the programming community, not those of the non-existent desktop publisher. Even by 1978 the use of computers for writing was sufficiently rare that the Apple II did not support lower case characters. As for telecommunications, in the 60's, phone links between computers (called "time sharing") were in their infancy.

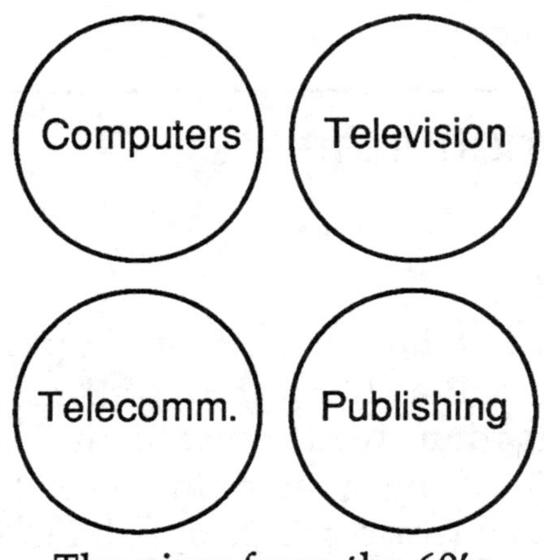

The view from the 60's

Today the world has changed quite a bit. The overlap between television, computers, telecommunications and publishing has started. From today's perspective, the drawing would look like this:

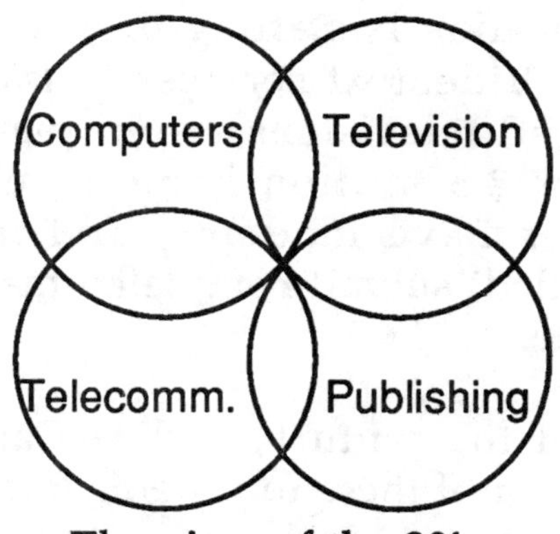

The view of the 90's

Old-line publishers were, in many cases, taken by complete surprise when desktop publishing hit the scene. The flurry of self-published books and newsletters had an impact on publishers as authors took a more active role in the overall design of their books.

The publishing overlap with television takes many forms, the most obvious of which is the creation of printed books to supplement major PBS series such as the Moyers/Campbell *Power of Myth.*

The overlap of computers with television takes several forms as well. Computer graphics and special effects are seen by virtually everyone every day. The technology needed to create the first 30 seconds of the introduction to the TV show *Jeopardy* used to occupy an entire room. Now it can be created with a desktop computer using tools like the NewTek Video Toaster. Even the home video hobbyist is creating computer-based titles using simple graphics programs and a hookup from an Apple II to a VCR.

Telecommunication is starting to overlap with all of these areas. Videotext services linking computers, telephones and televisions are in place around the world. Over 2.5 million home computers in the United States have modems, and many authors (myself included) submit completed manuscripts over the phone line.

By the end of the century, Ted McCain predicts the complete merger of these four fields into one.

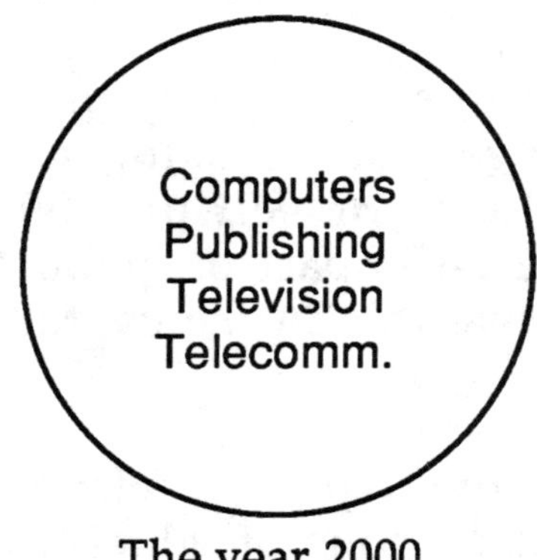

The year 2000

The trend is obvious. Look at products like Commodore's CDTV, or the CD-I offering from Phillips – these technologies extend the television metaphor to provide access to computer activities, and promote the publication of works on CD-ROM. Video trade magazines are starting to contain articles on the impact of multimedia on the video production business. The worlds of video and computers are merging at a fast pace.

Where's the TV? I need the phone to check my mail. The link between television and telecommunication is growing so strong that the regional Bell operating companies might get squeezed hard by the TV cable companies.

According to an article by George Gilder in Forbes, 60% of our homes are connected to cable, and 33% more can be connected very easily. Once this happens, TV cable hookups will rival phone hookups in the US. But TV cable has one important feature distinguishing it from normal phone lines.

The connection to your telephone is made with two wires called a twisted pair. These wires are designed to transmit low bandwidth signals associated with the frequencies of the human voice. Typically, these phone lines have a bandwidth of about 4 kilohertz. Television cables, on the other hand, have enormous bandwidth by comparison – one gigahertz. To grasp the difference, consider this: The entire Library of Congress could be sent over a television cable in under eight hours. It would take over 500 *years* to send this amount of information over a conventional phone line.

The problem with television cables is that the signals lose strength over long distances, requiring that amplifiers be placed along the way from the cable office to the home. This makes two-way communication over TV cables difficult.

But all this is changing as cable companies are installing fiber-optic lines. The motivation for conversion is two-fold. First, the loss of signal strength in fiber is so small that intermediate amplifiers are not needed. Second, fiber-optic cables can carry even more signals than traditional cables. Some communities (Queens, New York, for example) now receive over 100 channels of cable TV as a result of this new technology.

What does this have to do with telecommunications? Well, think about this. The phone companies currently have more fiber in the ground than the cable companies, but cable companies are switching over as fast as they can. And, even though the phone company fiber is in the street, that extra capacity doesn't do you much good unless you have high-bandwidth cable in your house. The only people who've managed to put that infrastructure in place are the cable companies.

Don't be surprised to see your cable provider offering phone service soon. TCI (the largest cable company) has formed an alliance with McCaw Cellular to develop a wireless phone service using cable.

In the meantime, if you want to see technomerge in action, you might want to examine X•Press X•Change – a cable-based information service that brings newswires and more into your home or classroom computer over the TV cable or satellite.

This service crams the contents of numerous wire services (AP, TASS, Xinhua, Kyodo, and many others) along with classroom guides to CNN and other television offerings, some pubic-domain software, shareware, and financial information onto a special channel that can be received through a one-way modem. This device extracts the coded information from your cable at high speed and ships it to your Apple II, Macintosh, or PC-compatible where it can be accessed with the X•Change software provided with the modem.

This information service is part of the basic cable offering in many areas – you may already have the X•Press signals coming into your school. (You should call your local cable provider to see if they carry this service, and let them know that you want it.)

Access to this wealth of information with an Apple IIe requires a Super Serial card (or other serial card). The Apple IIc, IIc+ and Macintosh computers have the serial ports built in, so nothing needs to be added here. (Hardware problems in the Apple IIGS prevent this machine from working with the system.) You'll also want a printer, although you can save the information you've received on disk. Any PC with a spare serial port should work, and files are saved in standard ASCII text format for use with virtually any word processor.

Once you've established a cable connection in your classroom (often provided for free, or at minimal cost), call your cable provider again to see if they will donate the cable modem to you as well. It never hurts to ask. Some cable services, like TCI and Heritage, sometimes provide up to 2 complete setups (modems, cables, and software) per school site at no cost!

But even if you have to pay for the modem, it is pretty

reasonable – under $100 (including cables and software) for the PC and Apple II versions, and about $125 for the Mac version.

Once everything is set up, the software lets you establish categories for information that you want to retrieve – weather, news, etc. The more categories you choose, the faster you'll run out of storage space, but you can trade off breadth for depth by customizing the information stream you want to receive by extracting, for example, only local weather, or news from a specific area. Once this is done, your computer will scan the headers of each incoming story to see if it fits one of your categories, in which case the story will be downloaded. At any time, you can browse through the stories that have already been received and print them out or save them to disk. As you delete stories from the computer, space is freed up for more stories to be downloaded.

If you have an old Apple IIe gathering dust in the closet, you may want to dedicate a computer just for the X•Press service and leave it on all the time. Just be sure to have students frequently save and delete the RAM-based files to make room for new information.

Imagine the impact of this technology on a current events class. For example, news from TASS on the latest changes in the countries making up the former Soviet Union stream onto your classroom computer at the same time these stories are appearing in newsrooms throughout the world. Students can collect stories, discuss which ones are newsworthy, and create their own daily newspaper. That night, students could watch the evening news to see how the networks dealt with the same information. Because wire services from many countries are represented, students get to see how each culture may interpret a given event in its own way – coloring the story as they cover it.

Wait – there's more

Macintosh users can download software that is also sent on this cable service and can even receive a multimedia database (the Media Centre) which will feature a catalog of cable programming as well as interactive classroom activities supported by color images and sound. In the future (as bandwidth increases), these services might support QuickTime videos for the Macintosh, further fuzzing the boundaries between telecommunications, television, computers and printing.

There are other technologies, not yet invented, that will provide other forms of merger among these four areas, of this we can be sure.

Meanwhile...

Now, what does this have to do with Roger's comment about the VCR being the printer of the 90's? Well, for one thing, if we believe that multimedia reports are going to become as commonplace as typed or written reports were when you and I went to school, then the VCR tape is the only cost-effective delivery medium currently available to the general public.

Everyone has a VCR – well, almost everyone. According to the Electronics Industries Association, by

January, 1991, 74% of the households in the US had VCR's. (A pretty staggering number, given that 14% of the households exist below the Federal poverty level.) Actually, this number is not a surprise. When I was working in Brazil, I found that even the poverty-stricken people who live in the poorest of conditions have VCR's.

One of the important features of a VCR is that, in addition to playing back tapes, it can be used to record. This places the means of "printing" in the hands of everyone with a VCR, assuming they have a video/audio source to connect to the recorder.

The Apple IIGS, because it supports color video adapted to the United States (NTSC) standard, connects to this "printer." Reports created in HyperStudio can be recorded at school for home viewing, teacher archives, etc., just by pressing a single button on a machine most of us use almost every day.

Now, here is an interesting question. If the future is one in which publishing, computers, telecommunications and television have merged, how do today's computers stack up?

Almost everyone would agree that the Mac is a perfect tool for producing printed documents. I have access to quite a few types of computers in my studio, and I rarely write anything more than a letter on anything except the Macintosh. The Mac virtually defined desktop publishing, and for good reason. The WYSIWYG (what you see is what you get) interface for word processors and page layout programs has always been one of the its strong points. The Mac and a laser printer (the printer of the 80's?) are a magic combination.

Desktop Presentations: Less Than Meets the Eye

As a tool for desktop presentations, the Mac and MS-DOS computers have a design flaw – their video output options. The only Apple products that support NTSC video are in the Apple II line. The Macintosh line either provides no external video connection at all, or it provides RGB (red green blue) analog signals that can be displayed only on expensive monitors. Most MS-DOS machines suffer from the same problem. The rationale for this choice is obvious. The NTSC video standard is incapable of displaying high-resolution images clearly. This situation is improved somewhat by the S-video standard showing up on high-end consumer equipment. But if you really want to see high-quality small text on a screen displaying a zillion colors, then high resolution, high-bandwidth (and high-cost) video monitors are the only way to go today.

If an NTSC capability had been designed into the computers most of us use today, then desktop presentations would be easier to display. While industrial training sites may have high-resolution multi-sync video projectors available, school classrooms do not. This constrains the Mac or MS-DOS computer to the role of a personal tool rather than making it into a presentation tool for the whole class to look at at once.

To see an example of paradigm paralysis in action, into

at the popular "desktop presentation" products on the market today. Most of them put more energy onto facilitating the creation of 35mm slides or color transparencies than they do in putting snazzy color pictures on the display screen. Some of these products do such a poor job of creating pretty screen images that they are barely worth opening. But this failure reflects adherence to a paradigm that says, in effect, "Presentations are done with slides and transparencies." This nifty relic of 50's thinking may comfort those who scan the channels for I Love Lucy reruns, but the rest of us are ready to enter the 90's with both feet. If the computer can let us design the slides, then why can't it be the primary presentation tool?

In fact, it can be. I haven't given a presentation with traditional slides since the early 80's, and I haven't used a transparency in five years. I give about 100 presentations a year throughout the US and Canada, and every one of these is completely computer-based. My reasons for doing this are simple: the computer is the best presentation tool I know of. If I find that my presentation is listed under a different title than the one used in my presentation, a minute during my setup time is all I need to create a new title screen. I use about 50 images per hour (counting progressive reveals, and other special effects unknown to most overhead transparency users) in my talks. My computer and display plate is a lot easier to carry on tour than 30 slide trays. The only problem with my setup is that the only high resolution display plate I could afford is monochrome. I'd gladly trade resolution for the ability to put my images on a color

TV monitor.

Products that perform the video conversion from the computer image to a standard TV image do exist, but they tend to be fairly expensive. High quality video converters cost $2,000 or more. Fortunately, the price point is dropping rapidly. For example, Prolab manufactures an inexpensive device called the VideoMaster. This small box works with MS-DOS computers to convert the VGA video signal into a standard composite (or high-quality S-video) signal for use with TV monitors or VCR's. This product retails for only $250 and, for its price range, it does a tremendous job,

Ultimately, the option of providing standard video output along with higher-resolution signals should be built into every computer shipped.

I'd like to see better slide show tools designed for the 90's, but until other computer manufacturers get as serious about video as Commodore has with the Amiga, there is no real market for the product I want.

If we were to create an image of the Macintosh or most MS-DOS computers today (without external video adapters) it might be drawn like this:

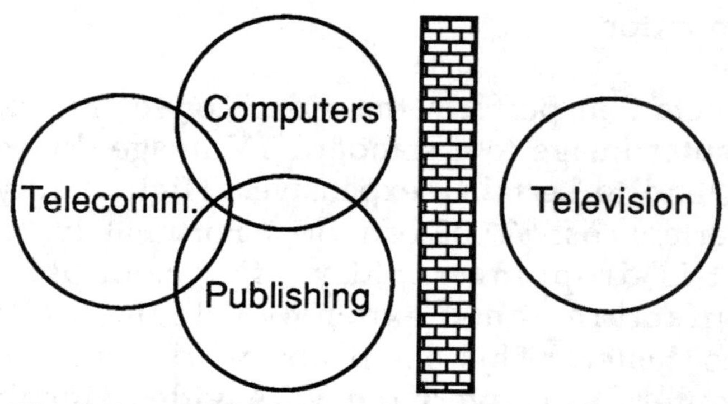

The Macs and MS-DOS machines of today

An interesting property of the future is that, like a fast moving train, it is coming our way no matter what. Those of you who are connecting your old Apple II's to your VCR (or taking advantage of add-on video conversion boxes for your MS-DOS or Macintosh computers) are riding the wave of the emerging paradigm. You are part of the integrated future.

MTV Comes Home

Those who are not experiencing the future yet should drop into your local Radio Shack store, pick up some cables and hook an Apple IIGS up to the family VCR for some experiments. If you need help with this, call Roger Wagner (619-442-0522) and ask him how to do it. He has a flyer showing how to connect your Apple IIGS (or any Apple II) to any VCR. If you are using the Prolab VideoMaster with your MS-DOS computer, instructions and cables for VCR hookup are provided with the package.

While your computer graphic images or HyperStudio or other hypermedia applications are playing, record your voice on the audio track of the videotape. See what response you get, and notice how you feel working with what may be a new medium to you. After awhile, you may find that your VCR has moved to your printer stand!

❄ Educational Uzi's

At the 1992 Winter Consumer Electronics Show John Sculley announced that Apple was going to enter the consumer marketplace with a line of "personal assistants" – portable information tools designed to facilitate information retrieval and communication.

With this announcement, Apple is entering a field well known to Casio, Sharp, Sony and others who design for pockets, not just briefcases. The $250 Sharp Wizard OZ-8000, for example, is a pocket computer with 32 K of RAM, several built-in applications in ROM, and the capacity to accept external application cartridges ranging from games to a fax module. The Sony Data Discman is a complete CD-ROM information retrieval system that fits in a coat pocket and retails, with three discs (including an illustrated encyclopedia) for under $500. Pocket information tools are showing up like ants at a picnic, and there is no end in sight.

These products reflect a trend well known to the computer industry since its inception: Technology gets faster, cheaper, smaller and more powerful with time. Look at a pocket-sized computer like the Wizard and compare it with the Apple II+. Your getting twice the capacity at one-third the cost and (including monitor) less than 1/20th the weight. Pocket video games (like the Atari Lynx) even provide a color liquid crystal display in a hand-held computer for under $100 – less that 1/10th the price of the old Atari 800 computer it replaces.

The rapid growth of pocket-sized information appliances is the tip of the iceberg. Just as the laptop/notebook computer market is the fastest growing segment of the computer industry, palmtop devices will grow like wildfire as well. To start with, these new products are straightforward technological extensions of pocket-sized entries dating back to 1980. While the products of that era were limited to small display and memory capacity, they provided their designers with the opportunity to think about what could be placed in small packages. Now that the market for these products is exploding, we can expect the handheld category to grow like crazy.

Educational Impact

All of which brings me to the classroom.

Many educators remain resistant to technology use in the classroom. Excuses of limited access, high cost, etc., are now just that – excuses. Yes, change is hard, but it is inevitable. All educators, at all grade levels, must insist on access to technology, and must become fluent users of the tools of the information age. Technology-resistant teachers might be able to keep computers from getting through the front door, but they can't keep them out of children's backpacks. Technology resistant educators will find their students armed with educational Uzi's, while they try to compete with the equivalent of a pen knife.

For example, kids with Sony's Data Discman are already looking up factual information on Compton's Encyclopedia disc, and seeing it all on their private viewing screens. Teachers who believe in the primacy of "lecturing" are completely outgunned by these tools.

Students with pocket word processors are taking notes and preparing reports that, when uploaded to a desktop word processing system at home, will be turned into a finely crafted document in a fraction of the time it takes to create a first draft by hand.

The Luddites Return

How are educators to respond to the challenges of personal information appliances? One approach is to forbid their use. In the past year I've encountered many teachers who refuse to let kids use calculators for long division, or use word processors with spelling checkers. One friend told me that his son's teacher was upset because the child alphabetized his spelling list using the sort feature on a word processor, rather than doing it by hand. When the parent asked why his child needed to know how to alphabetize words (without a context), he was told that this skill was essential in learning how to use a card catalog in the library. The parent pointed out that none of the libraries in his town had card catalogs anymore – all the searches were done with a computer-based system.

Wistful glances at the past make for fine conversation among adults, but convey a completely different message to children. The message that technological ignorance conveys is that school has no bearing on reality. One might as well have teachers come to school on horseback dressed in armor, speaking Elizabethan English, or light the classroom with candles made by the students during recess.

We've sent spacecraft beyond the reaches of our solar system, yet we deny children access to calculators. What's wrong with this picture?

The ostrich response

Some technology-resistant educators think that, if they look the other way, the tools of the information age will dry up and blow away. This approach (unsuccessfully applied to printed books in the Middle Ages) will experience the same success of the attempts to ban television. Some teachers are watching the clock tick toward retirement, hoping they won't have to learn anything new. Others are just denying that any of the tools of our age relate to their task.

Well, if you believe that, look at this. We spend over $200 billion on education in this country each year. That is the size market that causes corporations to drool. Yes, one might argue that the technologies I described are a bit pricey today, but that won't be true a year from now. Just look at what happened in the past ten years, and then look at what happened in the previous ten years. The faster, cheaper, smaller, more powerful trend has been well in place for over two decades, and it shows no sign of letting up. Sharp, Casio, Sony and others are wildly interested in creating tools for kids, and these tools will be reasonably priced.

Where will it lead? Look at the blister-packed calculators at Walgreens (for about $2) and think about Hewlett Packard's HP-35 calculator that cost $495 when it came out 20 years ago. Products with the capacity of the Sharp Wizard will break the $20 barrier in five years – maybe less. This doesn't require a crystal ball, just a plotting calculator (or, for those who are still avoiding high-tech, graph paper and a ruler.)

Ignorance of the trend is no excuse. Computer companies can now easily forget trying to sell computers into the classroom – they'll go after the kids directly!

As one example, look at the new Super Nintendo system. This game machine is really a Trojan horse. It looks like a game machine; it plays like a game machine, but watch out. Sometime later this year, Nintendo will roll out an adapter complete with over 8 megabytes of RAM and a CD-ROM drive for about $200. This means that, for well under $400, kids will have a complete multimedia workstation. You can be sure that keyboards, mice and modems won't be far behind. If I'm right in this prediction, Apple and IBM will just be transient blips on the face of personal computing unless they respond strongly, and respond fast.

Where does this leave the educator

It would be nice (I guess) if technology didn't move quite so quickly, but that just isn't in the cards. We live in a world of unprecedented change, and the rate of change is accelerating away from us at the speed of light. Educators can ride the trends by taking an active part in the revolution. They must get their hands into the fray and work with the technology themselves. To do otherwise is to risk having school become completely irrelevant in the lives of our students.

❄ Telecommuting to School

Have you ever watched children waiting for a school bus on a wintry day? Think about the hours spent standing in the snow, building memories they will share with their children, just as our parents did with us.

One of the trends in society these days is towards telecommuting – working from home a few days a week, using a computer equipped with a modem to perform office work. If this model works for business, how about for schools?

My son, Harvey, is a student at Harvey Mudd – one of the Claremont Colleges in Southern California. During his first semester I wrote to him several times, but never received a letter in reply. "Why didn't you write?" I asked during the Christmas break. "Dad," he said, "if you want me to write you need to give me your e-mail address."

Talk about paradigm shifts! I was operating from the world of quill pens and green eyeshades, and my son was thinking like a citizen of the late 20th century. We found that we could communicate through Internet (my address is dthornb@atl.CalState.edu) and we have chatted quite often since then.

I guess the point here is that Harvey and other post-Sputnik children are comfortable with the communication tools of our age. It makes me wonder what these students think when they sit in classrooms without telephones connected to the outside world. During a period punctuated by rapid global changes, our classrooms are isolated caverns locked from the very reality we are supposedly preparing our children to face.

Put a modem and computer in the hands of most kids, and they will quickly find connections worldwide. School-based projects (like KidsNet and Apple Global Education) are wonderful starts, but think about where this could go! If each school or district had its own bulletin board service (BBS) and provided access to local libraries, teacher "mailboxes," school announcements, public domain software libraries, etc., then students could never again complain that they forgot to bring the homework assignment home. If a student is ill, he or she could still do assignments and file them through the school's computer system. Kids could collaborate on projects over the phone lines, and teachers could lead discussion groups on topics related to class.

Telecomputing could open the schools to the entire community. Engineers at the local company could tutor kids at night on physics and chemistry. Others in the community could stimulate discussions on current events, tell stories, and so on. Because the phone line hides the age of the participants, cross-age discussions would flourish. Through telecomputing, schools would become true community resources.

To give a personal example of how this might help, I was speaking for a district in the Cleveland Ohio area when a major snowstorm hit. The schools were closed because the roads were blocked. Had this district been telecomputing with the community, teachers could have created discussion groups from home, with students dialing it from wherever they were. As it was, a day was lost.

Projects taking advantage of the home/school connection are already in place in Indiana, Illinois, Texas, Virginia, and elsewhere, and I expect this is just the tip of a trend that will flower in the next year or two.

The limiting factors:
One of the limitations to telecomputing is equipment access at home. While it appears that one out of four teens has a computer in his/her bedroom, I don't know how many of these are connected to modems. But when you consider that 2400 baud modems are available for well under $100, and 1200 baud modems are practically being given away, the issue of home access is rapidly being addressed. Virtually all laptop and notebook computers (including the lower-priced

models) have built-in modems. Rumor has it that the next generation of video game products from Nintendo will have a built-in modem. Telecomputing is quickly coming of age. While equity of access is (and will continue to be) an issue that should concern us all, we as a nation can easily afford to equip every child with a home computer system with a modem.

A greater limitation comes from the adult population who (like myself) is so conditioned to physical documents (such as letters from my son) that electronic communication catches us by surprise. What does it mean for a teacher to distribute homework assignments by computer? What tools will teachers use to "mark up" rough drafts of student work when no physical copy of that work exists? How will schools accommodate the number of phone calls streaming into the site each day as students, teachers, and others take advantage of electronic communication? These and other questions need to be addressed. At first, many faculty members will be squeamish at the prospect and many reasons will be advanced for not doing anything. But, if these reasons are examined closely enough, they will probably all boil down to one underlying reason: change is discomforting.

An even greater change...

If home/school telecomputing is threatening to some, then imagine how threatened we might be with telecommuting. Telecommuting – literally going to work through the phone lines – is a trend starting to emerge in industry. A growing number of workers operate out of their homes either full-time, or for several days a week. Improvements in user interfaces to telecomputing systems makes it possible for people to be productive wherever they are. You, for example, don't know if I wrote this chapter in my Monterey office, my San Carlos office, on an airplane, or in my home. You neither know nor care if this book was submitted by mail, AppleLink or through Internet. As the author, I don't even care which computer captures my text – all I care about is the task itself.

While social interaction is a valuable component of education, and physical contact between student and teacher plays a very important role – especially in the early grades – the role of schools might change remarkably if telecommuting was a reality.

Rather than have assigned classrooms, for example, the school site might become a huge resource center where students, teachers and others could mingle, conduct research, discuss projects, and interact freely. The structure of classes and assignments would be provided through telecomputing. When viewed in this manner, schools would change quite a bit. For starters, everyone at the school would be there because they wanted to be! The school site would bustle with excitement and activity. Students would complete their assignments and file them for review and grading, and teachers would be free to interact with students on a more personal basis. When appropriate, lectures would be scheduled, and many of these might be put on community access cable channels for those unable to attend in person.

The greatest change is that schools would become

places of learning and discovery, not institutions to house the young and provide custodial care for 6 hours a day.

Yes, but does it work?

On a recent trip to Indiana I had the chance to learn about a most innovative educational technology program. The Buddy System, incorporating 15 schools, places computers with modems in the homes of all children, grades 4 through 12. This saturation of technology represents, in my opinion, the only way we will insure that computers are used effectively in education.

This project is truly revolutionary because of the sheer volume of technology that has been installed. Families are provided with financing programs to pay for the equipment, and those who are unable to afford technology either have it given to them, or have their costs offset with financial aid.

The results to date are fascinating – the quality and depth of fifth-grade writing assignments has improved markedly, parents are learning to use the technology themselves, and, in some cases, the student's computer provided the incentive for parents to improve their own literacy skills. While the program has been in place for too short a time to measure its effect on dropout rates and test scores, several students have demonstrated astounding increases in their academic performance once they had unlimited access to a word processor. Given the national education agenda's focus on improved academic performance, adult literacy, and reducing the dropout rate, this one project shows what can be done for a very small investment.

Telecommunications is a critical component of the Buddy System. Homes are linked directly to schools electronically. Teachers post nightly homework assignments for students and parents to review. Electronic mail allows parents, teachers and students to discuss educational issues. Students "chat" with peers at other schools and collaborate on projects without meeting face-to-face.

Through network connections, students can reach remote information providers (e.g., Prodigy) for other information services.

As demand for this type of program grows, the carriers will have more incentive to replace our voice-grade phone lines with more powerful fiber-optic systems. These services should be in every community within a few years.

Expanding the dream

I've said for years that we should put a computer in the hands of every child in America. We, as a nation, can ill-afford to deny access to powerful information technology to all students, and the cost of providing this equipment is quite modest. Unfortunately, this recommendation has not received as much support here as I would like, although it has been adopted by Japan for implementation by the year 2000.

I'm of the opinion that we should stop horsing around and implement a program like the Buddy System (or some variant of it) for 4th through 12th graders throughout the country. I'm not suggesting that younger children can't benefit from computer access, only that, by the time children reach 4th grade, they should be as comfortable with telecomputing as they are with video games.

The neat part of this scenario is that it can be done today for very little money. Here's how it might work:

Let's assume the useful life of a personal computer system is 5 years and each child is to use a moderately powerful computer with a 40 megabyte hard drive, high resolution color display, 2400 baud modem, and an integrated software package for telecommunications, word processing, database, spreadsheet and graphics. An entire system with these capabilities can be purchased today for $800, tops.

Many parents would opt to buy the system outright. Those who wish could finance their purchase, perhaps through a local financial organization or, if needed, through a local or state-wide bond issue. If the purchase is spread over 5 years at 8% interest, the investment amounts to 53 cents per day – hardly a back-breaker for most families. But there are those for whom even this modest investment may be too much. Students who receive free lunches might receive free computers as well. Since the free lunch program costs taxpayers about $1.80 per day, increasing this amount by only 30% could provide a computer for these children also.

Those who want to increase the power of their installation could add a CD-ROM drive and a nice printer, bringing the total cost to 87 cents a day, based on current retail prices for single-unit purchases. Of course these prices would drop precipitously when vendors realize they are competing for the sale of 50 million computers in the first year alone. Imagine what this volume of computer sales might do for our economy!

The net cost (long-term) to the public would be only that for students taking part in the free lunch program, and for the equipment at the school site. This investment would be minuscule compared with the cost of other government programs such as the S&L bailout.

Changing education

An interesting consequence of projects like the Buddy System is that they provide an opportunity to rethink the structure of education. When subjects can be browsed and explored by students in their own way, many will have their native love of learning rekindled.

An article in the May 6, 1991 Tribune Star from Terre Haute, Indiana described the story of Deanna Overton, a sixth-grader who found school so difficult that she was failing most subjects a few years ago. Since the implementation of the Buddy System in her school in the 1988-89 school year, her grades have improved to the point where she is receiving A's and B's. Most importantly, she has a positive image of herself as a learner, and is actively engaged in school projects.

As Deanna put it, "This project has given me a head

start with my future. Those who don't learn about computers will be lost."

❄ Prometheus, Pandora and Thamus – Another Perspective on Technology

Some years back, I was of the opinion that, if only we could provide students with access to personal computers, education would automatically be transformed for the better. I held onto that belief for years, even though it was terribly naive and misguided. If all we do is bring technology into the classroom, there is no reason to think that anything positive will happen as a result. On the other hand, if we think carefully about the goals of education, and how technology can be used in support of these goals, then computers can be very useful.

Neil Postman is well-known for his views on the potentially negative consequences of technology on society, and on education in particular. His books, *Amusing Ourselves to Death* and *Technopoly* address this topic in depth.

I agree that there are many poor uses for computers (page turning software that provides students with context-free drill and practice, for example), and I also think there are a great number of very positive uses for technology in education. It is the positive side of technology that we must nourish and develop.

Underlying our concerns about technology (television, unlimited access to calculators, and so on) lies an important realization: technologies, once unleashed, have the capacity to change society – to facilitate paradigm shifts. This is not a new thought; it was known to the ancient Greeks, for example, through the stories of Prometheus, Pandora and King Thamus.

A story of Prometheus that relates to this topic takes place at the time when mortals were being created to populate the Earth. The Titan Epimetheus, and his brother Prometheus, were given the task of providing mortals with some means of protection. Epimetheus gave the slow tortoise a hard shell so he would be protected from attack. The tasty rabbit was given good eyesight and great speed, and the other animals were given their gifts as well to provide them with protection as was appropriate to their kind. Epimetheus was so generous that, when it came time to take care of mankind, nothing was left to give. Mankind had fair eyesight, but none nearly as good as that of his predators. He was given the capacity to run, but not to run very fast. He was denied thick fur to protect him against the elements. Humans, in short, were ill-prepared for life on the Earth, and this suited

Zeus just fine.

Prometheus felt that mankind needed a special gift and in order to assist these special beings. He flew to the heavens and stole fire – technology – from Zeus as a present for humankind. From this fire we could warm ourselves, cook our food, fashion metals into tools, and thus create our own protection from a savage world.

Zeus was furious. He had a mischievous woman made from clay, had life breathed into her, and saw that she was graced with incredible beauty. He arranged for this woman, Pandora, to be given to Epimetheus under the escort of Hermes. But, fearing a trick, Prometheus warned his brother not to accept this gift. Zeus flew into a rage and had Prometheus chained to a pillar where a vulture would pluck at his liver for eternity.

Eager to avoid a similar fate, Epimetheus married Pandora who, along with her beauty, brought less desirable traits. Pandora found a jar containing all the spites of mankind that Prometheus had hidden away – Old Age, Sickness, Labor, Insanity, Vice and Passion. Upon opening the jar, these all escaped, stinging Epimetheus and Pandora, and inflicting the race of mortals. Only Hope remained under the lid of the jar and did not fly away from her secure stronghold, for, as Zeus commanded, Pandora replaced the lid of the jar before she could come out.

Before commenting on this story, I'd like to share one from Plato's *Phaedrus*. In his dialog with Phaedrus,

Socrates explores the power of technology to facilitate paradigm shifts. Socrates relates the legend this way:

There dwelt at Naucratis in Egypt one of the old gods of that country, to whom the bird they call Ibis was sacred, and the name of the god himself was Theuth. Among his inventions were number and calculation and geometry and astronomy, not to speak of various kinds of draughts and dice, and, above all, writing. The king of the whole country at that time was Thamus, who lived in the great city of Upper Egypt which the Greeks call Egyptian Thebes; the name they give to Thamus is Ammon. To him came Theuth and exhibited his inventions, claiming that they ought to be made known to the Egyptians in general. Thamus inquired into the use of each of them, and as Theuth went through them expressed approval or disapproval, according as he judged Theuth's claims to be well or ill founded. It would take too long to go through all that Thamus is reported to have said for and against each of Theuth's inventions.

But when it came to writing, Theuth declared: "Here is an accomplishment, my lord the king, which will improve both the wisdom and the memory of the Egyptians. I have discovered a sure recipe for memory and wisdom." "Theuth, my paragon of inventors," replied the king, "the discoverer of an art is not the best judge of the good or harm which will accrue to those who practice it. So it is in this case; you, who are the father of writing, have out of fondness for your offspring attributed to it quite the opposite of its real function. Those who acquire it will cease to exercise their memory and become forgetful; they will rely on writing to bring things to their remembrance by external signs instead of on their own internal resources. What you have discovered is a recipe for recollection, not for memory. And as for wisdom, your pupils will have the reputation for it without the reality: they will receive a quantity of information without proper instruction, and in consequence be thought very knowledgeable when they are for the most part quite ignorant. And because they are filled with the conceit of wisdom instead of real wisdom they will be a burden to society."

From these stories we can properly conclude that debates on the appropriate use of technology reach into antiquity. Those who resist calculator use by students often make arguments similar to the one made by King Thamus against the written word.

There is one thing to consider, however. If Plato had not transcribed Socrates' dialog with Phaedrus, we'd probably never know about King Thamus' concerns!

Prometheus' gift to mankind is a sword with many edges. Technology can be used to enslave as well as to liberate the mind. Television's critics see this very clearly. As Neil Postman writes in *Technopoly*, "It is not merely a matter of tool against tool – the alphabet attacking ideographic writing, the printing press attacking the illuminated manuscript, the photograph attacking the art of painting, television attacking the printed word. When media make war against each other, it is a case of world-views in collision.

(We see this) most clearly in schools, where two great technologies confront each other in uncompromising aspect for the control of students' minds. On the one hand, there is the world of the printed word with its emphasis on logic, sequence, history, exposition, objectivity, detachment, and discipline. On the other, there is the world of television with its emphasis on imagery, narrative, presentness, simultaneity, intimacy, immediate gratification, and quick emotional response. Children come to school having been deeply conditioned by the biases of television. There, they encounter the world of the printed word. A sort of psychic battle takes place, and there are many casualties."

While there is much that can be (and has been) said in defense of this view, the time for argument has past. Television is ubiquitous, and computer technology will be soon. The difference between the two media is simply this. It is too late for educators (or just about anyone else) to radically alter the structure of broadcast television. The blessing of soon having hundreds of channels from which to choose is that television will truly provide programming for every taste. We can help parents and students become conscious consumers of televised materials, but the basic capacities, limitations, and uses of television are now cast in stone.

The relative scarcity of computers in today's classrooms means we still have time to influence how they can best be used to enrich the lives of students and teachers alike. In order to exercise this power, we must each take active roles in judging the appropriateness of software, and we must look carefully at the whole educational environment when exploring how best to make use of computer technology. If we sit on the sidelines, decisions will be made without our input.

Many decisions being made on software acquisition, for example, are driven by huge corporations who see children's minds as passive vessels to be filled with predigested material suitable for regurgitation on standardized tests. If you think this use of technology is inappropriate, you must speak up, and you must speak loudly. If you don't, there are others who will corrupt this technology for their own purposes, and we will have lost a golden opportunity.

Make no mistake about it; computer technology and interactive multimedia devices will become as commonplace as televisions within a decade. The time to act is now.

If you are frustrated (as I am sometimes), and if you think that nothing you say or do will make a difference, remember that Pandora's jar still contains Hope – and that we can choose to release this to the world ourselves!

❄ Multimedia and the Intuitive Learner

Upon this gifted age, in its dark hour,
Rains from the sky a meteoric shower
Of facts ... they lie unquestioned, uncombined.
Wisdom enough to leech us of our ill
Is daily spun; but there exists no loom
To weave it into fabric...

Edna St. Vincent Millay

If we think about the rate at which the volume of information is growing, we see that this fragment of Millay's sonnet describes the major challenge of the information age – how do we create informational retrieval systems that allow us to make meaning from the sea of data that threatens to engulf us? In short, how can our information tools let us explore conceptual space at the speed of thought.

Today's high school science student is expected to master information that was taught at the college level ten years ago, and may have been unknown twenty years before that. So fast is the rate of information growth that, in the sciences, some have estimated that half the information being taught will be outdated in five years. In addition to the need to be updated with new information, the sheer volume of knowledge is growing exponentially. The meteoric shower of Millay's poem rains down upon us all. The good news is that the loom to weave it into fabric does exist today – it is the CD-ROM.

To illustrate the kinds of information being distributed in this form, World Library, Inc. has placed over 950 classic works of literature (with illustrations) on a single disc, with room for even more. Imagine the works of Homer, Heraclitus, Aristotle, Kant, Chaucer, Darwin, and many hundreds of other authors – all on a single disc that can be searched in seconds for any reference. A traditional library collection of these volumes could scarcely fit in most homes, yet the CD-ROM version can be mailed across the country for less than a dollar. In addition to the economy of storage, libraries of this type have a singular advantage to the researcher: one search for words and ideas can span the entire library so that a query on justice, for example, will reveal treatments on this topic from authors as diverse as Plato and Arthur Conan Doyle.

The diversity and depth of information available in this format is formidable. For example, NASA has placed many thousands of high-resolution images from the Voyager mission on a series of CD-ROM's that can be carried in a coat pocket. The collection of the National Portrait Gallery is available on CD-ROM, as are numerous other libraries of cultural and scientific information. A child with the right CD-ROM's has access to more information than was in the Vatican library at the height of the Renaissance.

Until recently, access to information in this format required a desktop computer with a CD-ROM disc drive. With the introduction of the Sony Data Discman, information access moves with the user. The Data Discman is a complete CD-ROM information delivery system that fits in a coat pocket and retails, with three reference works, for under $500.

And so we not only have an explosion of information, but an explosion in the accessibility of this information. Increased access, while essential in this time of rapid change, is not enough. The CD-ROM contains data – not knowledge. It is the function of the human being to convert this information into knowledge that can be used in some purposeful way – to use the technological loom to weave the raw data into a fabric that then becomes a magic carpet with which we can journey into the realm of meaning at the speed of thought.

This is, in fact, a fairly new issue in the world of informatics – especially in the consumer marketplace. One pioneer who had the courage to tackle this problem head-on was Vannevar Bush, President Roosevelt's science advisor. In an article appearing in the July 1945 issue of The Atlantic Monthly, Dr. Bush forecast the advent of hypermedia databases that worked by associative rather than by more linear searching methods. The technology needed to implement his vision was not available at the time, and his paper is all the more valuable because it helped to shape some of the major ideas about computer access to information in use today.

More recent commentaries and extensions of the ideas in Bush's paper by Ted Nelson and by Gabe Ofiesh (see references) provide the logical extension of these thoughts.

While the volume of information has been exploding exponentially for at least a century, it is only within the past few years that access to this information has been made less cumbersome. For example, at the time of Mendel's experiments with peas, scientific publication was occurring at such a prodigious rate that his results went undiscovered for over a generation. Now we can find anything we want in a flash – and we have to think about what this means for those who want to find meaning in all this data.

* * *

Our own work in this area has led us down some non-traditional paths, so we beg your indulgence as we explore a different approach to this problem.

User-interface designer, Aaron Marcus, once said, "The user interface is the mask; the tasks are the rituals." Anyone who has used a computer certainly has experience with the ritualistic quality of most tasks.

Commands are issued in a certain sequence – data must be saved before turning off the computer, etc. There are many ritualistic tasks that we perform with computers every day. As for the user interface being a mask, the goal of effective computer software is to trick the user into forgetting about the computer altogether – to step through the looking glass, so to speak, and "touch" the application. My word processor presents me with a paper white screen on which my text is placed as if typed by a typewriter. And yet the image I see is nothing but a pattern of dots that are carefully positioned so as to trick my eyes and brain into thinking that I am working with a physical document.

This mask-like aspect of interfaces becomes apparent when done poorly. Word processors that require arcane commands to format a document, or that otherwise interfere with the writing process, are less effective than those that support a consistent metaphor for the task at hand. Programs that make you wait while responding to a query disrupt the flow of thought and interfere with the user's creativity.

Bush's ideas on searching by association created a metaphor – or mask – whose purpose was to make the computer operate in ways that mesh with the ways human beings think. All of which brings to mind the tale of the man who went to the computer console and typed in the question: "Do you suppose that computers will someday think like human beings?"

After a pause of several minutes, the computer printed out its answer: "That reminds me of a story."

If you were amused by this tale, it was probably because you know that storytelling is (so far as we know) a uniquely human experience. For thousands of years mankind has learned around a fire. We are still learning around fires today although, more often than not, the glow comes from a television or computer display screen – not from the embers of a log.

A concern that we might have about this modern "fire" is whether or not it is being used to tell stories effectively. Well-told stories have several characteristics that we can see in this one collected from the Santa Clara pueblo in New Mexico.

There is a telling of the time before the two-leggeds walked upon the surface of Mother Earth when Thought Woman sent Coyote up to the surface through a hole in the ground. Coyote had a leather pouch strapped to his back, and was instructed to run south as fast as he could, and to never open the pouch.

Coyote ran and ran, and after a time grew hungry for there was little on the Earth that he could eat. At long last he stopped and took the pouch from his back. "Perhaps this pouch contains some food," he thought. He opened the pouch and saw that it was filled with stars – all of which immediately escaped and flew into the sky where they reside to this very day.

Thought Woman was furious with Coyote, so she gave him a toothache. Each night, for thousands of years, Coyote would sit and stare at the stars he had released, and howl in pain. Other animals grew afraid of Coyote for, when they approached, they too became ill – all except for Field Mouse who rubbed some herbs on Coyote's cheek to take away the pain.

Think about this story for a moment. What is it about?

In all likelihood you can find several things that this story is about. You might decide that it is a creation myth describing how the stars came to appear in the sky, and why coyotes howl at night. Or you might decide that it is a story about the awakening of consciousness – the light of awareness, and that it shares much in common with the Promethean myth.

The point is that this story (and most well-told stories, for that matter) is about all of these things at the same time. Western culture, at least since the time of Descartes, has been treating the cognitive and affective domains of experience as if they were separate (and separable). We see this in education when we talk about these areas separately, rather than treating them as an integral whole. In my opinion many of the challenges we face in education today can be made easier if we rekindle storytelling and storymaking in our teachers and learners alike.

The holistic quality of stories helps account for their engagement. Whenever I start to tell a story, the mood of the audience changes; it becomes more focused, more engaged, more open to what I have to say. In the world of education, there is little that could be more powerful than storytelling – and storymaking.

There is another aspect of stories that make them important tools for education in the United States today. We are experiencing a growth in the population of people from diverse cultures. The education of people from distant lands requires more than sensitivity to their native tongue; one can be fluent in English and yet be influenced most strongly by one's native culture. Stories – especially old stories that resonate with our primordial past – are culturally independent. I have found tales from the Pueblo Indians, for example, that are exact replicas of stories told by the Sufis in the twelfth century.

Some multimedia products on the market today, like the Voyage of the Mimi series, are effective because they tell a story. If you watch the video tapes from either voyage, you'll find a story that explores science, math, human interactions, the nature of questing, and many other topics as well. These are all integrated in a way that keeps the viewer engaged. The ancillary materials associated with these videos were designed to focus primarily on the science and math aspects of the programs, but educators are free to explore the other topics as well.

One of the great powers of multimedia is that it allows storytelling on a grand scale. But this aspect of multimedia must be designed into the product – it does not emerge by virtue of the medium alone.

The twelve-stone medicine wheel becomes a talisman for effective storytelling; the path from South to North is that of the Body, and the path from East to West is that of the Spirit. A complete journey takes both paths.

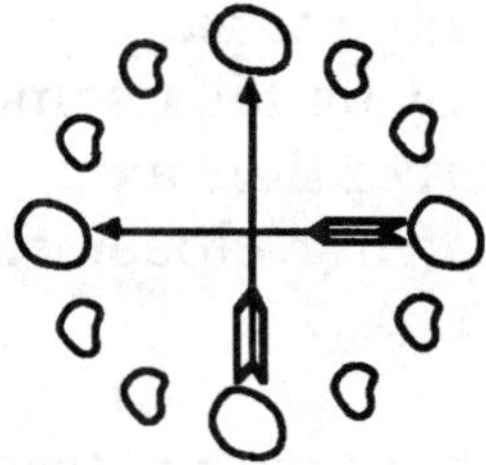

The mandala symbolism, found in the medicine wheel, fascinated Jung because of its universality across time and cultures. His studies of archetypes led him to create mandalas of his own to express various modalities of human behavior.

In the world of education, Dr. Bernice McCarthy has created her own medicine wheel. Because of its impact in our thinking about the design of multimedia learning environments, we'll spend some time discussing McCarthy's work before applying it to the task of facilitating the exploration of conceptual space at the speed of thought.

Her goal was to understand the nature of individual learning styles so as to help teachers create environments in which all can learn with equal ease. In McCarthy's cosmology of the mind there is a distinction between how we perceive and how we process information.

The domain of perception has, at one end, the sensing or intuiting of information. In other words, if you perceive at this end of the spectrum, you operate from a gut level or inner sense. The other extreme is conscious thought. Perception at this level is rational.

Of course it is unlikely that any of us is at one extreme or the other. Each of us falls somewhere between the extremes of the perception axis, although we might find ourselves hovering closer to one end than the other.

Next we'll explore how we process information – how we make sense of what we perceive. Again, there are two extremes. On the one end is "watching." If you fall at this end of the spectrum, you most likely learn well by seeing something demonstrated by someone else. The other extreme is "doing." If you fall at this end of the processing axis, you'll find yourself learning best by jumping into the activity itself and trying it out on your own. As with perception, each of us falls somewhere between the extremes on the process axis, perhaps hovering closer to one end than the other most of the time.

Now, if we take both axes – the perception and the process lines – and place them at right angles to each other, they create the basis for a mandala with four quadrants. Each quadrant defines the domain of a particular learning style. While you may visit all the quadrants at one time or another, there is probably one in which you feel most comfortable. For example, if your approach to learning a new computer program or other high-tech tool is to jump in and start playing without even opening the manual, then you are operating in the fourth quadrant – sensing and doing.

An important point about McCarthy's work needs to be made at this point. It is NOT her goal that learners are exposed to approaches from only one style. On the contrary, she feels that everyone should be exposed to information presented in a way that touches on all four styles. In the process of exploring information through all styles, everyone gets to shine part of the time, and everyone has the opportunity for insights that come from the other styles of learning.

To understand how this model relates to education, we'll explore each of the four styles in order.

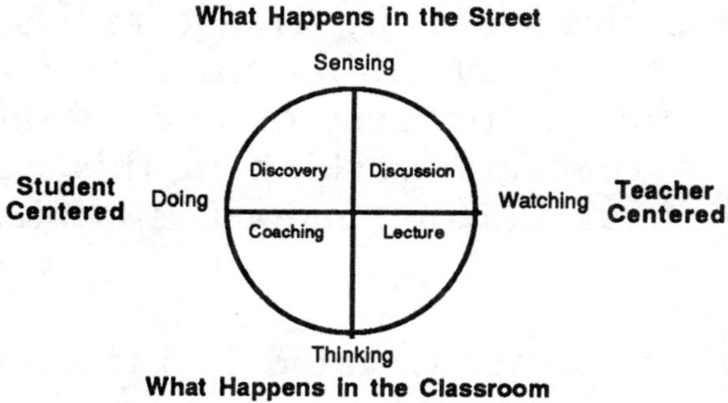

The Type I learner (located in the upper right quadrant) is the imaginative learner who prefers to learn through sensing and watching what is happening in her world. This person's favorite question is "Why?" The teacher needs to create a reason – a rationale for the exploration of the subject. The teacher's role in this quadrant is to be a motivator.

The Type II learner (located in the lower right quadrant) is the analytical learner who prefers to learn through watching and thinking about what is being presented. Traditional classrooms are set up well for this person. As an informational sponge, this learner's question is "What?" The teacher is the presenter of facts – an information provider. It is worth noting that, while these learners shine in the typical lecture-based classroom, McCarthy estimates that they represent, at most, 25% of our students.

The Type III learner (located in the lower left quadrant) brings us from the "watching" side of the circle to the "doing" side. This is the common sense learner who prefers to learn through thinking and trying ideas out. Engineers often fall in this category. A common question from this learner is, "How does this work?" The goal is to try something out through direct experience for the purpose of understanding it rationally. Teachers working in this quadrant encourage experimentation and act as facilitators or coaches.

The Type IV learner (located in the upper left quadrant) is a dynamic learner – someone whose motto might be "Ready, Fire, Aim!" These are the people who never read recipes, instructions for assembling garage door openers, nor are they willing to ask for directions when they are lost. They just charge into the abyss, making their own way as best they can – learning a great deal in the process. By operating through intuition and direct experimentation, this learner is often thinking, "What can this become?" Teachers of these students need to let them teach themselves and others, and to function as a resource to the student and as an evaluator of her work.

As you might gather, people who operate in diagonally opposite quadrants often have a hard time learning from each other. The student who learns best through direct instruction often has the hardest time when thrown into a situation requiring the intuitive working out of an idea. I've seen many graduate students who performed extremely well in their coursework, but who completely fell apart when they had to design and carry out their own experiments for their thesis projects. The shift from from second to fourth quadrant was just too big a jump for these people to make.

Looking at McCarthy's model in another light, the top two quadrants describe what happens in the street, and the bottom two describe what happens in school. On the street, intuitions are of paramount importance, and in school, logical thought is valued above all else. I've seen this manifested in the extreme in Brazil where children are very bright and largely intuitive learners. Many thousands of these children live on the street, surviving through their instincts. Yet their classrooms are modeled on the most rigid European model of lecture and recitation. It is little wonder that over 80% of the Brazilian children leave public school before completing the eighth grade.

If we were to bring more of the "street" ways of perception into our own classrooms by honoring intuitive, sensing perception styles more, we might have fewer children identified as "at-risk."

Continuing with this broader look, the right two quadrants (those involving watching) suit teacher-centered approaches to education, while the left two quadrants support student-centered approaches.

Plutarch once said, "The mind is a fire to be kindled, not a vessel to be filled." This quote favors the left side of McCarthy's diagram.

Of course there is a place for all types of instruction, and while it is exciting to think that teachers can teach around the circle, touching each quadrant in turn, many educators are so locked into their own dominant style that they have a hard time relating to the needs of learners whose styles are very different from their own.

✱ ✱ ✱

What does all of this have to do with multimedia and computer software in general?

I think that one of the hallmarks of a really good instructional program is that it allows the user to navigate through the world of information at her own pace and in her own style. One example of this that comes to mind is the *Geometry* program for the Macintosh from Brøderbund. This program provides highly interactive support for a high school course in plane geometry. While the program is structured to conform to the presentation format of standard math textbooks, and can be followed in a linear step-by-step fashion, it also allows users to browse through topics at will, stopping to explore anything that looks interesting.

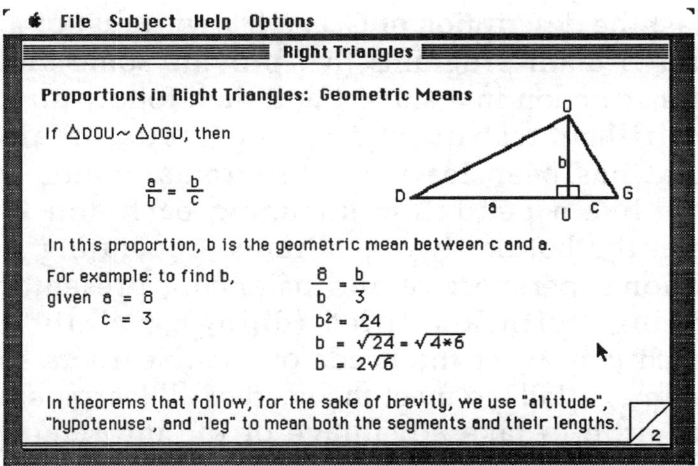

Intrepid explorers will even find that they can go to screens "before the beginning" to explore additional math activities that are not directly related to the subject.

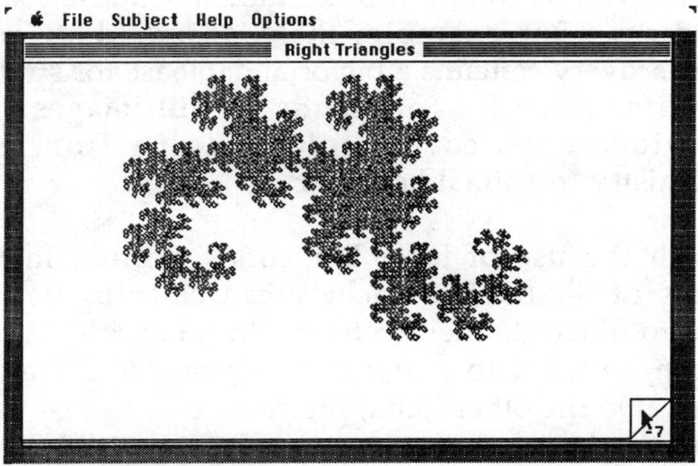

The careful design of this product shows a rare attempt to balance sensing and thinking, watching and doing.

Contrast the description of *Geometry* with that of most structured math programs that provide some limited direct instruction in a subject and then follow up with some drill or test questions to establish that the material has been learned. Programs of this type operate like a pendulum swinging back and forth between the bottom two quadrants – operating from the rational perspective and balancing presentation (watching) with activities (doing). While this approach may meet the needs of some learners some of the time, it fails to meet the need of all learners, and it does little to take advantage of the informational tools of today.

Unfortunately, while well-balanced programs like *Geometry* exist, they are few and far between.

Examples of open-ended tools that support multiple pathways can be found in other media including laser videodiscs. For example, the *BioSci II* disc from Videodiscovery contains a pictorial database for studies in the life sciences. Thousands of still images and short video clips cover topics ranging from cell biochemistry to animal behavior.

Through the use of laser bar codes printed in the margins of textbooks, teachers can call up specific images to illustrate their lectures. In other words, this disc can be used to support traditional lectures in biology. On the other hand, the same disc can be used by students in an unstructured exploration of the rich pictorial database. Learners can browse and build their own pathways through this visual library. The disc itself is neutral – it can be repurposed in a variety of ways. A teacher who wants structure can restrict student access to its use as a supplement to prepared texts. At the other extreme, the teacher can provide a broad challenge – the creation of a video report of endangered species, for example – and students can search for the images they want to incorporate in a multimedia report of their own design and construction with no further intervention from the instructor.

Another way to use laser videodiscs for open-ended problem solving is demonstrated through Videodiscovery's *Science Sleuth* disc. This videodisc contains 26 problems presented through scenarios. The problems range from people getting sick at a picnic (what is making them ill?), to an accident between a bicycle and a car (who is at fault?), to the mysterious case of the exploding lawnmowers. Using the laser bar code wand, users can play the vignettes, research relevant topics and look at resource materials to gather clues and formulate hypotheses on the problem's solution. At no time is the user told what the "right" answer is.

These vignettes create a story that unfolds completely under the user's control. The class discussion resulting from these problems sets the structure for the problem solving. Many pathways can be chosen through the information, depending on the class strategy for getting to a satisfying resolution of the challenge.

The beauty of providing multiple pathways through a

subject is that it allows students to learn in their own style. In addition to helping them understand material better, this has the additional benefit of keeping students engaged with the learning process – letting them maintain the spark for learning with which they entered school.

The challenge of multiple access pathways becomes amplified when we enter the world of the CD-ROM. Because of the immense storage capacity of this medium, CD-ROM's are often used as repositories of information – pictorial databases, encyclopedias, collections of magazine articles, etc. There is much value to using this medium in this way. The challenge is how we can take advantage of the computer to help us navigate through a vast amount of information purposefully, quickly, and in a way that honors our unique way of making meaning out of raw information.

To illustrate the challenge that faces us, let's take the *Magazine Rack* CD-ROM as an example. This disc contains the full text of one-year's issues of 300 magazines covering subjects including health, business, technology, and numerous other topics. Rather than providing "all the news that's fit to print," this disc holds all the news that fits. The user interface for this disc is quite serviceable. Users are asked to pick a broad category to search, and can then conduct a variety of detailed searches on author, topic, or even conduct a word search based on the text of the articles themselves. The search process is quite rapid and, if the user has a clear idea of her goal, this product can save many hours of research in the library.

Suppose our goal is a bit broader – to explore different ways that a particular topic was treated in the press by various magazines. In addition to the ability to rapidly search through all the articles for reference information, the user would benefit from having other tools to facilitate the journey. These tools might take the form of agents who would ask stimulating questions or pose challenges.

So far, user interface design has focused on making computers easier to use by basing the interface on familiar metaphors. I'm proposing that this idea be extended – that the metaphors governing new user interfaces be based also on how we prefer to acquire and process information. This means, rather than providing just one pathway through vast realms of data, that multiple pathways be supported.

* * *

One day Coyote was running home through the woods. He soon came upon a fork in the road. To his left the path was barren. The trees were dead and the road was strewn with rocks. Even the sky above this path looked gray. The path to the right was quite different. The trees were green, birds sang from the branches, and colorful flowers sprouted from the fresh moist earth underneath a beautiful blue sky.

Coyote chose the path on his right, and trotted along, looking at the pretty colors and enjoying the smell of the fresh flowers. However, while he was admiring the beauty surrounding him, he fell into a deep pit.

As he looked up at the sky from the bottom of the pit he said, "I'm so happy I took the beautiful road. After all, if something this awful could happen to me here, imagine what would happen if I had taken the barren path."

In the world of computer access to information, all journeys are mediated by metaphors. For example, Macintosh users are familiar with the desktop metaphor in which programs and data files are kept in folders placed on a simulated desktop. The user opens folders and can select programs or files for use by clicking on these objects with a mouse. The metaphor of the desktop provides a familiar context to the user, thus simplifying the task of using the computer.

Metaphors are of great value, but they also limit our choices. This aspect of metaphor was explored in depth by Marshall McLuhan. In particular, he proposed that, whenever we create a metaphor we achieve four things:

1. The creation or enhancement of something new,
2. The obsolescence of something old,
3. The retrieval of something from the past,
4. The flipping or reversal into a new paradigm (setting the stage for its own destruction).

For example, let's apply this model to the metaphor of desktop publishing. Desktop publishing does these four things:

1. It makes everyone a publisher,

2. It obsoletes the typewriter,
3. It retrieves the medieval interest in typography,
4. It sets the stage for hypertext and multimedia publishing.

If we talk about user interfaces for multimedia tools, we run a risk if we base our navigational metaphors on documents – on the Gutenbergian idea of left-right-top-down arrangement of information. McLuhan's notion that every metaphor is a four-edged sword is important. If our goal is to facilitate natural access to information in ways that make meaning for the user, then our metaphors must be empowering in each of their four aspects.

I'm going to propose something fairly radical. Since we are creating metaphors for navigating through conceptual space, then let's take our guidance from the universality of ancient stories and look at primordial metaphors. The reason for going as far back as possible is that, if each metaphor is based on the ones that preceded, then newer metaphors are likely to be more restrictive in their power than older ones.

If we take multimedia-based stories as our metaphor, for example, then applying McLuhan's model we achieve:

1. The technological magic carpet for the mind,
2. The obsolescence of a fractured curriculum,
3. The retrieval of our tribal past, rekindling the deep knowing imparted to our cells over the eons spent listening to elders speak around the fire,

4. The setting of the stage for individuals becoming constructors of their own knowledge.

How far back can we go in designing our story? What is the primordial metaphor? It must be existence itself. Oral traditions from around the planet agree on the essence of the creation of consciousness – the *logos* or word found in the Sanscrit: "In beginning is the Word," or *Nada Brahma* (The World is Sound), the first line in the Gospel of St. John; all these refer to the vibrations that separated chaos into order. The primordial light of Hesiod, Genesis, and hundreds of other writings all point back to the beginning of metaphor and story.

And so when we sit around the fire to hear a story, the light and warmth of the flame rekindles the deep memory of the birth of creation.

One glimpse of what must have been the very beginning is provided by Chuang Tsu in his *Inner Chapters*:

If there was a beginning, then there was a time before that beginning. And a time before the time which was before the time of that beginning. If there is existence, there must have been non-existence. And if there was a time when nothing existed, then there must have been a time before that – when even nothing did not exist. Suddenly, when nothing came into existence could one really say whether it belonged to the category of existence or non-existence? Now I have said something. But I don't know whether what I said has said something.

If this is your first reading of this passage, you might well ask if what he has said has said something. I believe that Chuang Tsu was trying to reach back to the very beginning – that he was searching for the primordial metaphor. Personally, I find it significant that he was working on these ideas around the time that Lao Tsu was writing the *Tao Te Ching.* When Jung developed his theory of archetypes, he was amazed to find that many of his ideas were already known to the ancient scholars, but had been hidden from the view of Western eyes for centuries.

While working on this topic I had lunch with a friend at a Chinese restaurant. My fortune that day said, "The philosophy of one century is the common sense of the next."

McCarthy's work on learning styles connects smoothly with the ideas of Jung, and thus with the work of the ancient philosophers who were looking for primordial metaphors. For that reason, I think that navigational metaphors based on her four quadrants may provide an effective vehicle for navigating through the vastness of conceptual space.

As an example of how this might be done, imagine a large domain of information such as the type being put on CD-ROM's today. In addition to the normal browsing tools that we have come to expect in such products, the computer will also keep track of the user's journey. At any time the user can backtrack, leave markers or notes, and can save this path for reentry at a later time. At the same time, the user has access to four agents – animals that act as guides through the exploration of the subject. Each of the four animals represents one of the four quadrants of McCarthy's model.

The four animals were chosen by exploring numerous traditional stories. The animals are Hawk (Type I), Field Mouse (Type II), Beaver (Type III), and Coyote (Type IV). Based on the traditional stories, each of the animals was chosen to align with one of the quadrants in McCarthy's chart. Hawk intuits and watches and is interested in the big picture. Field Mouse watches and thinks, pays attention to detail and is wise. Beaver thinks and acts, has a plan and carries it out. Coyote acts and senses, but rarely thinks. Coyote stumbles into danger without a plan. Fortunately, Coyote reincarnates.

To illustrate how these agents might appear in a program, imagine an application built around Aesop's Fables. The program contains a hundred or so of these fables that can be read in any sequence the user desires. After reading a fable, the user can select one of the four agents for assistance. Hawk might encourage exploration of the variety of animals used in the stories, and ask why animals were chosen as the main characters. Field Mouse might present the moral of the story and then ask what you might conclude from this moral. Beaver might ask you to create your own moral, or write your own fable based on the structure of the ones you had been reading. Coyote might do anything. You might get sent into the midst of *Beowulf*. You might be sent to a fake fable. You might be given the chance to examine the structure of the program itself. Coyote might even remove all structure and let you write a letter to a friend, or send you on your own with no guidance at all.

At any time, the user is free to choose and change agents. The goal is to facilitate the exploration of ideas in any way that is natural for the user.

Edna St. Vincent Millay was right when she said, "Wisdom enough to leech us of our ill is daily spun." The loom to weave it into fabric exists in the form of CD-ROM's, laser videodiscs and other multimedia tools. Our goal is to provide the pattern for the loom in the form of a user interface that turns the resulting fabric into a magic carpet to carry us across the boundaries of space and time into the infinite universe of the mind.

❄ Changes – What Needs to Happen?

The structure of the traditional six-period day is better suited to teacher-based didactic presentation rather than to a more student-centered approach to learning. School sites should be free to experiment with extended periods to allow more in-depth exploration of content. Other educational models, such as integrated thematic curricula, afford other possibilities to make education engaging to all learners. These and other approaches should be freely chosen by educators on a site-by-site basis.

While the move toward site-based management is positive, it is unlikely to have any lasting positive effect if the decision makers at the site are unaware of the various options available to them. Toward this end, it is essential that, as power shifts to the site, educators are provided with opportunities to learn about various restructuring models so they can make informed choices.

Insofar as technology is concerned, release time is essential if educators are to master the use of informational tools. In addition to increased release time to attend educational technology conferences, technology-using educators need to be able to work with their peers to share their knowledge on the practical uses of these tools in the classroom. Fortunately, effective models for on-site technology training exist and the challenge is finding effective ways to disseminate these models to all schools in the country. For example, the SuperSub program developed by Kam Matray of the Monterey Model Technology School Project in Monterey, California, provides early retiree's with a substitute teacher curriculum that can be brought into classrooms to free the principal teacher for one-on-one training. This approach has been quite successful. Teachers who are afraid to explore technology in the presence of their peers can work with a staff development person without fear of looking foolish if a program doesn't load properly.

Changes in Facilities

Many of our schools are falling apart. Many thousands of children are housed in trailers as school enrollments have outraced the community's ability (or willingness) to build new schools. Assuming that enlightned taxpayers will provide the resources needed to bring our schools into good physical condition, this also provides us with an opportunity to design and build schools in ways that acknowledge technological advances beyond the slate chalkboard.

For example, every classroom should have sufficient electrical outlets to support universal access to computers by students. This means at least a duplex outlet at each desk and network cabling. The teacher's work area needs to be supported by at least six outlets to support a computer, printer, laser videodisc, VCR and other A/V equipment needed in the classroom. Assuming that rearview color projection systems are unlikely to be placed in schools on the basis of space constraints, minimal provision should be assured for ceiling mounted video projectors. This requires sufficiently strong ceiling beams to support a color video projector along with at ceiling-mounted power outlet and a cable race to bring the video signal from the teacher's work center to the projector. The description just provided represents a minimal implementation and can be enhanced for those educators wanting to use additional technologies.

Just as the 16mm projector has become an anachronism, the blackboard may be the next to go. An appropriate compromise in classrooms for the next decade would be to have chalkboard panels on either side of a high-gain projection screen. This would allow educators to supplement their use of instructional technology with traditional hand-written comments.

Making Change Happen

For the vast majority of teachers, the two issues limiting technology use will be access and education. Of these, education must be addressed first. Rapid changes on the technological horizon suggest that, unless educators first understand the utility of the devices being brought into their classrooms, the technology risks becoming outdated while teachers try to figure out how (or why) to use it. This suggests that intensive and ubiquitous access to staff development on the proper uses of educational technology become a high national priority.

Once educators understand both why and how technology helps the educational process, access to this technology needs to be provided – along with sufficient release time for educators to restructure lessons in ways that take advantage of these tools.

Both education and access are continuing rather than one-shot issues, so staff development in these areas needs to be ongoing, just as it is in industry. The cost of doing this job properly is minuscule compared to the cost of lost opportunity to our nation if we fail to properly equip students for life in the 21st century.

Recommendations

Because existing technologies are continuing to undergo rapid change, and new educational technologies appear on the horizon with great regularity, it is recommended that educational technology policy remain flexible so as to be able to accommodate new technologies as they become available. In order to maximize the benefit afforded by new technologies into the foreseeable future, it is also recommended that:

1. regular reports are generated and widely

disseminated to apprise education policy and decision makers of new and forthcoming technologies;

2. educational technology budgets maintain flexibility so that purchasers are free to explore new technologies as they appear;

3. states continue to fund model technology projects with school districts and with software developers to help incorporate the latest advances in technology with existing state frameworks in the curricular area, much as California is doing;

4. staff development programs bring educators up to date on all aspects of educational technology, providing not only awareness, but access to these technologies for incorporation into the classroom if teachers so choose. This educational program needs to start in our preservice programs, but must be supplemented by annual updates in keeping with the rapid growth of technology.

5. Some provision needs to be made for multi-state credentials for educators using distance-learning tools (satellites, etc.) This will become increasingly important as two-way video conferencing moves us beyond the realm of the "talking heads" presentations facilitated by today's satellite systems. As one example of the challenges facing us in this area, should Dr. Carl Sagan be allowed to "teach" astronomy to our K-

12 students, even though he is not a credentialed teacher?

6. The issue of fair use of copyrighted information for classroom use needs to be addressed – especially the repurposing of video in multimedia projects. Today many teachers operate in total ignorance of copyright laws, freely showing recorded television broadcasts to their students, and freely allowing students to incorporate clips of copyrighted video materials into their own reports. Even the digitizing of images from videodiscs for inclusion in computer-based hypermedia reports may violate the copyrights of some information providers. Rather than address these issues, many educators bury their heads in the sand, arguing that their use of these materials is educational, and that this gives them license to do what they want.

   While this argument may have appeal to some, it runs counter to a strict interpretation of the law, and – sooner or later – the whole notion of "fair use" needs to be addressed. The fact is that much of copyright law was drafted prior to the advent of modern informational technology. The place for this discussion, hopefully, is not in the courtroom, but in a venue that supports collaborative rather than adversarial proceedings. The longer we wait, the greater the risk that adversarial proceedings will strongly hamper effective, rational discussion of this topic.

This brief list of recommendations can and should be supplemented by you. For in the final analysis, it is up to each of us to effect change in our communities. Some educational leaders think it is too late – that we have too far to go in the time allowed. I disagree. The revolution is at hand; *let's work together to make it happen!*

❄ References

Introduction

Marvin Cetron and Owen Davies, *American Renaissance: Our Life at the Turn of the 21st Century* St. Martins Press, 1989.

Education at Risk

A Nation at Risk, USDOE, 1983.

America 2000: An Education Strategy, USDOE, 1991.

Jacques Attali, *Millennium: Winners and Losers in the Coming World Order*, J. P Tarcher, 1991.

The Business Roundtable Participation Guide: A Primer for Business on Education, National Alliance of Business, 1991.

C. C. Carson, et al., *Perspectives on Education in America*, Unpublished briefing paper, Sandia National

Laboratory, 1991.

Ina V. S. Mullis, et al., *Accelerating Academic Achievement: A Summary of Findings from 20 Years of the National Assessment of Educational Progress,* Educational Testing Service, 1990.

Nan Stone, *Does Business Have Any Business in Education?,* Harvard Business Review, March-April, 1991.

Susan Tifft, *A Crisis Looms in Science,* Time Magazine, Sept. 11, 1989.

Al Wrigley, *Chrysler Seeks Japan Presses for Canada Unit,* Metalworking News, April 30, 1990.

What Does Business Want from Education?

The Business Roundtable Participation Guide: A Primer for Business on Education, National Alliance of Business, 1991.

Ira Magaziner, et al., *America's Choice: High Skills or Low Wages!,* National Center on Education and the Economy, 1990.

Vouchers and the Death of Public Education

John Chubb and Terry Moe, *Politics, Markets, and America's Schools,* Brookings Institution, 1990.

David Kearns and Dennis Doyle, *Winning the Brain Race: A Bold Plan to Make Our Schools Competitive,* Institute for Contemporary Studies, 1988.

Jonathan Kozol, *Savage Inequalities: Children in America's Schools,* Crown, 1991.

Nan Stone, *Does Business Have Any Business in Education?,* Harvard Business Review, March-April, 1991.

Education for the 21st Century

John Naisbitt and Pamela Aburdene, *Megatrends 2000: Ten New Directions for the 1990's,* Morrow, 1990.

Phillip Schlechty, *Schools for the 21st Century,* Josey-Bass, 1991.

K. Sheingold and M. Tucker, eds., *Restructuring for Learning With Technology,* Bank Street College of Education, 1990.

Alvin Toffler, *Future Shock,* Random House, 1970.

Alvin Toffler, *The Third Wave,* Morrow, 1980.

The U.S. Consumer Electronics Industry 1991 Annual Review, EIA, 1991.

When I Was My Child's Age – Paradigm's Lost

Joel Barker, *Future Edge: Discovering the New Paradigms of Success.* William Morrow, 1992.

Present Tense and Future Perfect

Thomas Armstrong, *In Their Own Way,* J. P. Tarcher, 1987.

Arthur C. Clarke, *Profiles of the Future,* Holt, Rinehart

and Winston, 1984.

Stanley Davis, *Future Perfect*, Addison-Wesley, 1987.

S. Davis and B. Davidson, *2020 Vision: Transform Your Business Today to Succeed in Tomorrow's Economy*, Simon & Schuster, 1991.

Howard Gardner, *Frames of Mind*, Basic Books, 1983.

Dudley Lynch and Paul Kordis, *Strategy of the Dolphin: Scoring a Win in a Chaotic World*, Fawcett, 1988.

Magazine Rack CD-ROM, Information Access Co.

Bernice McCarthy, *The 4MAT System: Teaching to Learning Styles with Left/Right Mode Techniques*, Excel, 1987.

Faith Popcorn, *The Popcorn Report*, Doubleday, 1991.

David Thornburg, *Education, Technology, and Paradigms of Change for the 21st Century*, Starsong Publications, 1991.

Alvin Toffler, *Powershift – Knowledge, Wealth and Violence at the Edge of the 21st Century*, Bantam Books, 1990.

The Death of Textbooks

For a catalog of CD-ROM's conatining NASA images, contact the Space Science Data Center at the Goddard Space Flight Center, Greenbelt, MD.

The Library of the Future CD-ROM, World Library Corp.

Technomerge

George Gilder, *Cable's Secret Weapon*, Forbes, April, 13, 1992.

Ian Jukes and Ted McCain, *Living, Working, and Learning in the Culture of the 21st Century*, 1992.

X•PRESS Information Services, contact Steve Landsiedel at 800-7PC-NEWS.

Educational Uzi's

V. Hugo, *Hunchback of Notre-Dame*, Book 5, 1831.

M. McLuhan, *The Gutenberg Galaxy: The Making of Typographic Man*, Univ. of Toronto Press, 1962.

M. McLuhan, *Understanding Media: The Extensions of Man*, Signet, 1966.

Telecommuting to School

The Buddy System can be contacted at One North Capitol Ave., Suite 925, Indianapolis, IN 46204, or by phone at 317-231-7145.

Prometheus, Pandora and Thamus – Another Perspective on Technology

Plato, *Phaedrus*

Neil Postman, *Amusing Ourselves to Death: Public Discourse in the Age of Show Business*, Penguin

Books, 1985.

Neil Postman, *Technopoly: The Surrender of Culture to Technology,* Alfred A. Knopf, 1992.

Multimedia and the Intuitive Learner

Vannevar Bush, *As We May Think,* Atlantic Monthly, July 1945.

Bernice McCarthy, *The 4MAT System: Teaching to Learning Styles with Left/Right Mode Techniques,* Excel, 1987.

Marshall McLuhan and Bruce Powers, *The Global Village: Transformations in World Life and Media in the 21st Century,* Oxford, 1989.

Edna St. Vincent Millay, *Collected Sonnets,* p140, Harper and Row, 1988.

Ted Nelson, *Computer Lib/Dream Machine,* Microsoft Press, 1987.

Gabe Ofiesh, *The Seamless Carpet of Knowledge and Learning,* in *CD-ROM: The New Papyrus,* Microsoft Press, 1986.

Chuang Tsu, *The Inner Chapters.*

Changes – What Needs to Happen?

For information on the SuperSub program conducted through the Monterey Model Technology Schools project, contact Kam Matray, 408-655-5012.